(*continued from front flap*)

for his first carving and, on his return from World War I, arranged for him to go to Leeds School of Art. Later, in London, he became a student and then an instructor at the Royal College of Art, and, during the thirties, launched that extraordinary sequence of evolving forms from which all his later production has derived.

In 1940, when air raids drove Londoners to shelter in the underground stations, Moore sketched in pencil and water color the rows and rows of reclining figures. These drawings were exhibited in 1942, and the tide of appreciation turned. By the fifties his commissions and honors abounded. Ultimately he turned down a knighthood, saying that if the day began with his assistants saying, "Good morning, Sir Henry," he wouldn't be able to work at all.

The logical culmination of Moore's preceding work is the great sculpture recently installed in the North Plaza of Lincoln Center. Sixty years of experience and experimentation have shaped that reclining figure, and those years of learning and doing are remarkably evoked in these pages.

HENRY MOORE

Books by Donald Hall

HENRY MOORE

The Life and Work of a Great Sculptor

By DONALD HALL

With More Than 100 Photographs and Drawings

HARPER & ROW, PUBLISHERS

A large part of this book, in somewhat different form, appeared originally in *The New Yorker*.

FIRST EDITION

LIBRARY OF CONGRESS CATALOG CARD NUMBER: 66–15732

for Philippa

Contents

A Note

I would like to thank first, and most of all, Henry Moore, who has been generous and helpful beyond any biographer's legitimate hopes; who has patiently answered several thousand questions in interviews and letters; who has searched out and provided photographs, and has even read my text to look for errors of fact; and Irina and Mary Moore, who have been consistently hospitable and charming. My wife Kirby has been an invaluable editor, reading and rereading material with which she was already familiar, and has helped with many interviews as well. For various kindnesses I would like to thank Geoffrey Hill, James Gindin, Marvin Eisenberg, William McClure, Edgar Riley, Alfred H. Barr, Jr., Edgar Young and E. P. Wilson. William Shawn, of *The New Yorker*, taught me a great deal about writing factual prose, for which I am most grateful. And Victor Perera, who was working in *The New Yorker*'s checking department at that time, helped me to avoid some embarrassing errors.

To the people of the following list I owe the bulk of my book; they are the old and new friends of Henry Moore, the art critics, gallery owners, collectors, bronze-founders, sculptors and painters who were kind enough to talk to me about Henry Moore: Mr. and Mrs. Raymond Coxon, Stephen Spender, Bernard Meadows, Barbara Hepworth, Sir Herbert Read, H. R. Fischer, R. V. Pitchforth, Constantine Fitzgibbon, F. W. Ambler, Sir Philip Hendy, Geoffrey Grigson, Sir Kenneth and Lady Clark, James Johnson Sweeney, Mr. and Mrs. John Thompson, John Russell, Eric White, Roland Penrose, Sir Frank Lee, H. Noack, Patrick Phillips, Isaac Witkin, Jane Wade, Harry Brooks, Rose Fried,

Martha Jackson, Lydia Winston, Lilian Somerville, Charles Gaskin, R. J. Kitaj, Eduardo Paolozzi, Robert Melville, Mr. and Mrs. Maurice Ash and Philip King. I am especially indebted to David Sylvester, who talked with me extensively, out of his great knowledge of Moore and of modern art, and later read my manuscript and provided corrections of fact and of implication. I alone am responsible for the errors which have endured despite the efforts of others.

D. H.

Ann Arbor
January 1, 1966

1

December 20, 1963:
The Locking Piece

HENRY MOORE gets up at 7:30. He makes a pot of tea downstairs in the kitchen (Yorkshiremen believe that no one in the south of England knows how to brew tea) and takes it back to the bedroom, where he and his wife Irina each drink two cups. At 8:00 they listen to the BBC news and weather. On December 20, 1963, he heard that the day would be fine, and he was pleased; bad weather had been keeping him from working outside on his big, new Locking Piece. He descends to breakfast and more tea at 8:30. If it's 8:35 and he has not yet emerged from the bathroom, Irina calls up the stairs, threatening him in her delicate Russian accent, "Henery, shall I make the tea?"

At breakfast there is the mail. Moore's feelings about the mail are ambivalent. He looks forward to it, and if there isn't a quantity he is disappointed, yet answering mail is the greatest tedium of his life. By this stage in his career, in his sixties, Moore is very rich and very famous; either condition makes for correspondence. Whole drawers are full of unanswered letters. Now and then he takes a day away from work, and dictates to his secretary; a week later he seems just as far behind. One morning there is a letter from *Harper's Magazine* asking him to write an article on Giacometti. A medical charity asks him to donate a sculpture. The Oxford University Press wants him to do an illustration for a book. Three dealers write for information about Henry Moores they have for sale. His tax accountant asks a question. An American Ph.D. candidate is interested in "the influence of vorticism on your work." Unlike many prominent men, he cannot leave letters unanswered. He will deny a publisher's request to do a book of lithographs, but deny it at great length, giving many reasons.

The Moores eat breakfast in the long dining room at the front of the house, a pleasant room full of paintings and flowers. Henry puts the date on the envelopes and passes to Irina the letters in which she might be interested. At 9:00 his sculptural assistants arrive and start to work in one of the new studios in the field behind the house. By 9:30 the mail is read and Moore intends to be at work himself, often in one of the small old studios in front of Hoglands—which is the name of the Moores' whitewashed, asymmetrical, fifteenth-century farm cottage. They moved here in 1940 from London, which is twenty-five miles

3

In back of Hoglands

away, to the hamlet of Perry Green, near the village of Much Hadham, in the county of Hertfordshire. To the right of Hoglands as you face it a series of sheds and outbuildings trails away toward the road. There is a garage for the Rover, and an open-ended shed housing a ping-pong table. Moore plays a rough game of ping-pong. He crouches at his end of the table with his eyes gleaming, shifting on the balls of his feet, and lashes out with an eccentric service. His backhand is good when he's set for it, but he has trouble moving the paddle over quickly enough. Sometimes instead of trying he strikes at it with his left hand, and occasionally his bare palm hits an ace. "That *counts*, doesn't it?"

Beyond the ping-pong shed are three old studios, his only studios until he bought more land behind the house in 1956. The first, a long, low, dark room, is now used mostly for patinating bronzes. Moore doesn't paint his sculptures as a lot of artists do, but his stone is always chosen with an eye to color, and now he colors bronze over a wide

4

range by swabbing it with chemicals and buffing it. A small middle studio is mostly a storeroom, full of tiny plaster maquettes and pieces of bone or flint. The third studio, which Moore calls "the far room," is the sanctum. He can only reach it by stepping outside the storeroom, among some shrubbery, and then up into the far room. From the road or from Hoglands, it is a doorless room, a secret place, like the imagination of the artist.

Moore doesn't plan his work schedule in advance; "I let the morning decide." The sunny December morning decided that he would work on the Locking Piece, but he would wait until the sun was higher. He would start by finishing waxes of small sculptures, in the far room. Moore's bronzes are cast by the lost-wax method, which requires a wax original of each bronze that is cast—ten waxes for an edition of ten. He must finish each wax himself, correcting minor deviations from his original plaster and sometimes adding marks which wax will take and plaster won't.

That December morning, he arrived in the chilly workroom just before 9:30, wearing a long blue-and-white striped butcher's apron. He lit a kerosene burner, and turned on a small two-bar electric heater. By ten o'clock the temperature had risen to 50 degrees. A meager winter light came through the transparent roof, and Moore used a gooseneck lamp to throw a special light on the waxes. He sat in a wicker chair, the wax in front of him mounted on a little turntable so that he could inspect all sides easily.

The far room is cluttered with a thousand objects, most of which have put in time on this turntable. There are plaster maquettes from twenty-five years back, including some tiny versions of the stringed figures of the late thirties—white bowls and baskets strung like harps. There are photographs of big sculptures on the walls, and there are shelves and shelves of bones, flints, pebbles—the natural objects which are sources of many of his forms—and small sculptures resembling bones, flints and pebbles. When Moore wants to modify, or add to, a bone shape, he makes a plaster cast of the bone and then builds on it. The room is a mint of forms, a magic closet. It's here that the new shapes—even a bronze thirty feet wide and sixteen feet high for the North Plaza of Lincoln Center—are born from a piece of flint and a pair of modeling hands.

In front of Moore that morning was the wax of a new helmet head in

5

Natural sources: pebbles and bones

two parts; the wax was a deep red, and the helmet looked like a red plastic toy for a Martian child. One part was the exterior shell, a sort of knight's helmet swelling out a little at top and bottom. The solid back looked like a woman's torso; into the hollow front fitted the second part of the sculpture, a slim standing trunk that branched into eyes at the top. Moore was adjusting the angle at which the internal piece stood, adding bits of wax to the base. He rolled the strips of wax between his fingers to make them pliable, and warmed a spatula in the flame of an alcohol lamp, then smoothed flat the added wax. Sometimes he could not find the tool, and glanced distraught over the jumble of surfaces around him, and blamed his assistants the way one blames a child for anything out of place.

The alcohol lamp flickered and went out. He stood up and stretched (working over these waxes is a sleepy, relaxing thing to do; he must pay attention, yes, but he is not *inventing*) and refilled his lamp in the storeroom next door. When he returned he ignited a strip of newspaper at the electric fire and started the lamp again. After ten minutes more of delicate smoothing, the helmet head was ready to go back to the founder and become bronze.

Then he began work on the wax of an upright figure, a totem pole-ish piece that needed adjustments to most of its facets. At ten minutes past ten there was a knock on the studio door. Mrs. Tinsley was sorry to disturb him but Mr. Jackson had come with the photographs. Mr.

Jackson entered with a stack of eight-by-ten prints. They were pictures of Moore at work in this room. Moore approved, and Mr. Jackson left to photograph the sculptures in back of Hoglands; he had waited until a sunny day to drive out from Hampstead.

Half an hour later Moore finished the upright figure and decided it was time for elevenses. Apron off, he walked back to the house and talked with Mary, his seventeen-year-old daughter, who was home that day, about the dance he was driving her to that night. Mrs. Tinsley had a telegram for him, and Irina was afraid there would not be enough milk for the coffee. Since the day was fine they sat on the sun porch at the southern side of the house, across the hall from the dark dining room. Henry Moore sat in masculine solitude among Irina, Mary, Mrs. Tinsley, Sheila the cook, and Mrs. Barber, the part-time cleaning woman. Then the phone rang for Henry—a friend had just returned from Los Angeles and wanted to tell him about his show there—and when he returned his coffee was cold.

By 11:15 the cookies were eaten, the coffee was finished, and everyone was back at work. It was time for Moore to visit the big, new studios at the bottom of the garden, where two of his assistants had been working since nine o'clock. He walked through the hall, past the stairs and the office, and between the old and the new living rooms. The end of the hall is a small gallery of sculpture and ceramics, mostly pre-Columbian and medieval English. Then he entered a glassed-in vestibule with doors on either side. To the right is the front of the house and the old studios; to the left is the garden and the new studios. The floor is thick with mats for foot-scraping, and under a bench is a row of Wellingtons—high English rubber boots to wear over socks—for visitors who take a muddy walk over the acreage behind Hoglands.

Henry Moore put on a sporty blue-checked coat, a soft checked hat turned down all around and blue mittens, and walked out the left door toward the new studios. Just past the vestibule is a greenhouse where Irina keeps her sophisticated collection of cacti. Farther on, fruit trees which Irina has espaliered mark the end of the old garden, after which the level lowers a few steps and the new garden begins. It is informal —borders of shrubs, annuals and perennials curving among hedges and trees. Here Irina Moore passes as many of her waking hours as she can. There is a living-in gardener for heavy work, but the garden is Irina's passion and her creation. The borders are in tune with the landscape and the season. In autumn the garden blazes with chrysanthemums and dahlias. In a corner of land five hundred yards from the house, Irina has planted bluebells where her husband leaves old plasters of large sculptures to break into unpredictable shapes. In the spring these fragmented white forms hover over masses of blue flowers.

Moore uses the new land partly as a private sculpture park. He keeps one copy of most of his bronzes now, and because they go off to exhibitions and come back again he walks past a rotating show of his work every time he visits the new studios. Today he walked past his King and Queen, that archaic pair of rulers, perched on top of a small hillock. A little further was a Glenkiln Cross, half cross and half torso struggling toward definition. Elsewhere were a seated draped figure and a warrior perpetually falling to the ground. As Moore passes them he notices different things: Maybe one of them has gone dead for him, and he wonders why; maybe another looks better in one kind of light, or from a particular angle. They give him lessons in sculpture.

At the end of the new land are the gardener's cottage, a cutting garden, a greenhouse full of potted begonias, fuchsias and datura lilies, and a vegetable garden. Nearby are the two new studios, brick with big doors so that large plasters mounted on platforms with tiny wheels can be moved outside. A miscellany of large bronzes stand on the platforms outside the studios, and inside are sculptures in various stages of

completion—from big bronzes awaiting patination to skeletal arma-
tures, the insides of what will become large plasters.

It is Moore's sculpture factory, complete with assistants as factory
workers. Traditionally, the master sculptor has workers to help him,
either young apprentice sculptors like Moore's assistants or professional
stone carvers, wood carvers or metalworkers. Rodin had thirty assistants at one time, as Moore is quick to say, and many of the better
modern sculptors have served their term as assistant to an elder. Moore
never did, and never had help until he was almost forty, but now he
cherishes assistance as a device allowing him to produce more sculpture. Today his assistants were Isaac Witkin and Ron Swan, with
Witkin more or less established as foreman. A burly, round-faced South
African, he has established a reputation of his own in London. Though
some assistants are unhappy in their work—it's just a job; you don't see
enough of Moore, who's always on the telephone, or sitting on a
committee in London, or showing visitors around the studios—others
like Witkin are enthusiastic. He doesn't want to be influenced by
Moore's forms but by his spirit. (Moore is conscious of the danger, and
never looks at his assistants' own sculpture unless he is asked; if they
know he won't be looking, they won't be tempted to try to please him.)

In the new living room

"Something of the man himself rubs off," and you realize "how green you are in form knowledge."

Of the five sculptures that Witkin had worked over in his two years as an assistant, the Locking Piece was his favorite. "I've never seen Henry so *involved* as with this one." The Locking Piece, in its final shape, is a generally circular bronze, nine feet high, in two parts which fit together like a child's puzzle. It doesn't resemble any one thing—it's not like the King and Queen, or one of Moore's family groups, which express the single image of their title—but it is full of different images as you walk around it, or focus on one facet or another. There's a portion of it which looks like an elephant's foot; there are scraps of landscape and of natural objects; there are bits and pieces of many faces, including a fragment of T. S. Eliot's nose. The more abstract a sculpture is, the more inclusive it can be of form experience. Walking around the completed Locking Piece, the observer encounters a series of soft explosions of recollection; forms become other forms, a hill from one angle is a torso from another, with a sort of wit in the sudden shift of scale. The Locking Piece is the end result of thousands of things seen and things touched.

Moore has some clear ideas about its sources. It began, like most of Moore's work, from his observation of nature. In digging the garden on

Another view of the Locking Piece

their newly acquired land, the Moores uncovered a graveyard of animal bones, an old butcher's depository. A good many pieces of sculpture have climbed out of that grave. One day, puttering among the bones, Moore noticed the way a joint fitted and worked. A short time later, as he was sitting idly, perhaps in conversation, his hands played with a pile of small stones. (Moore's hands are never still, and all over his house and studios are piles of objects—shells, flints, pebbles, crystals—for the touching.) Two stones accidentally locked, making a perfect fit.

These two incidents, coming close together, were the immediate genesis of the Locking Piece. However, there are always more sources —sources less conscious and anecdotal. First there is the artistic readiness, the liability to be stimulated by a particular natural observation: This was supplied by Moore's recurring abstraction, and by his recurring interest in sculptures made of more than one piece. Another ingredient, perhaps more common in the work of Henry Moore than in the work of most artists, is a connection to his childhood. He remembered, eventually, a device that he had known as a boy, not a locking puzzle, but a toy "bomb": You placed a paper cap between two pieces of metal and threw it on the sidewalk to explode. It fitted together like the Locking Piece.

Sometime in 1962, sitting in the far room at the little turntable, Moore made a maquette of the Locking Piece which was about four inches tall. In the process of shaping the clay, and turning the small construction about, his hands discovered and created innumerable small reminiscences of nature: the noses, the elephant's foot. If we ask what a nose has to do with an elephant's foot, Moore answers that all forms are grist to the sculptor's mill: "Likeness is richness." The more a piece contains of different things, Moore believes, the longer it will have interest for people. Whatever *is* just what it *is* loses its interest quickly. "You've got to have some sort of mystery." And the different shapes all have meanings: "The way an elephant's foot, soft, will lift up and fall down. It's not the form only. It's all you know of the strength of the elephant too." Form experience brings with it the associations of the form, a vocabulary of feelings.

Sometimes after a sculpture is finished, Moore will suddenly have a new insight into its origins or significance. Perhaps a year after the big Locking Piece was exhibited, and four years after the original

maquette, Julian Huxley invited Moore to his house in Hampstead:
There was something Moore had to see. In his garden Huxley had
placed, as a sculptural object, the skull of an African elephant—and it
closely resembled the Locking Piece itself; the hinge between jaw and
skull was the interlocking joint. Moore was delighted. He plans to cast
the skull in plaster, to have a copy at Hoglands. He had seen elephant
skulls at museums which he visited as a young man in his search for
natural forms. Stuffed elephants fill the entrance hall to the Natural
History Museum in South Kensington—perhaps the final discoverable
bit in the mosaic of sources for the Locking Piece.

After Moore made the four-inch maquette, he gave it to his assistants
to copy, but in a version three feet tall. That December day in 1963,
Moore and his assistants were working on the translation of the three-
foot figure into the nine-foot final version. This three-part evolution is

typical of the process of Moore's recent large sculpture. He needs to begin with a plaster or clay or plasticine sketch or a series of sketches. But enlarging always involves changing, and to go directly from four inches to nine feet (or fourteen feet, or twenty-eight feet) is usually *too* difficult. The distortions would be so enormous that revisions which could be made at the three-foot stage might be lost, and the sculpture spoiled or abandoned. In the case of the Locking Piece, the maquette was never cast and was destroyed, because the revisions in the three-foot version improved upon it.

Moore gives his assistants a working model and tells them the size he wishes the enlargement to be. They cover the model at its extremities with numbers representing the distance from a wooden frame which they move back and forth over it. Multiplying the distance from a larger frame, they build an armature, nailing together slim pieces of wood, and hanging chicken wire from the outermost ends. An armature looks a lot like wire sculpture; if the extremities of wood are numerous enough, it also looks like a porcupine. The wire of the armature is measured to be slightly inside the skin of the final sculpture, and the assistants then cover the wire with a thin layer of plaster, while Henry Moore observes their progress and directs revisions. When an assistant copies a maquette or model, constant small questions arise which require Moore's presence for a decision. Revisions in plaster are easily made, but when Isaac Witkin was carving an elmwood reclining figure for Moore, he had to consult him three or four times a day, since a mistake could have been irrevocable.

The three-foot Locking Piece was cast and exhibited, but Moore intended all along to make the large version. The large Locking Piece is far more effective than the small one. Size can be meaningful or expressive, for one thing. As Moore says, a mother-and-child figure of life size, or less than life size, is a tender object. Make them thirty feet tall and they become terrifying. The Locking Piece is a head only abstractly; instead of being terrifying at nine feet, its facets are liberated. It becomes less a head and more a repository of other forms: The elephant's foot takes on its shape and feelings, the landscapes and faces free themselves from the matrix.

But the large version is not simply an expansion of the small one. When you blow up a small sculpture it is always necessary to alter proportions slightly. To begin with, they have to change in order to appear the same, because the new height of the sculpture changes the angle from which the viewer sees it. Also, the twenty-seven-fold increase in volume produced by tripling the dimensions has the effect of making the lines more subtle as well as more monumental, and the big piece requires new decisions in the relationship of line and volume. One modification of a line will alter three perspectives, perhaps a nose, a chin and a mountain. What is convex from one angle may be concave from another, and the shift may be a triumph and may be a disaster.

One of the admirers of the small Locking Piece was the architect Gordon Bunshaft. Moore told him in October, 1963, that he planned to make the big version, and Bunshaft had the idea that it would suit a new building of his, the Banque Lambert in Brussels. The Banque owners were interested, but wanted to see the Locking Piece *in situ* by the start of February, 1964. Having begun in October Moore could not possibly have had it cast and patinated by February; but at least he could, by hurrying, finish the plaster, paint it bronze-color and transport it to the site for inspection.

To make the large version, Moore's assistants started all over again, with measuring marks on the three-foot piece and a huge armature.

Assistants at work on armature

This time the plaster would be too large to cast in one piece; it would have to be sawed into several pieces for casting, and so the armature could have no nails or wire. They tied the sticks together with ropes, and draped cheesecloth from the extremities instead of wire. By December 20, the large Locking Piece looked already finished, a huge white copy of a small bronze original.

But it was not. Work had fallen behind because bad weather had kept Moore from rolling it outside to have a good look at it. It was impossible to make crucial discriminations inside the studio, where you could only stand a few feet from the plaster. Today Moore and his assistants opened the big shed doors and pushed the Locking Piece onto the concrete, wedging crowbars under the wooden platform it rested on. The white shape dazzled in the winter sun. For two hours Moore studied it from all angles and distances. His assistants moved it around full circle, a few inches at a time, and moved the three-foot model along with it. They shifted a cardboard background to cut off interference from other bronzes outside the studio. After Moore had stared hard at the two Locking Pieces from each new angle, he started giving directions for revision, sometimes making rapid pencil sketches in a notebook while Isaac Witkin looked over his shoulder. Ron Swan stood to one side, listening, not speaking.

The language was simple. "We need to take the wobble out of our line." "If we have that bit curved out that way, don't you think it makes it difficult to join it to that piece up there? We have to curve it *in*, so it will make a join for that other piece up there." "That's a flat surface. It's going over *that* way too much." "That we were talking about before as being too curved, it's too curved from here too." "This gets wider, you see, and I wanted it to. I want it to look as if it gets wider all the way to the top. This one gets narrower." "Go down on that side and file it down there." "Our curve at the top there isn't flat enough. This corner wants to go higher. That is, this should go off straighter here, before it begins to curve."

There was much talk about weak and strong. "Take the calipers to the little bronze and then to the big one, and see if it comes out three times. It looks too weak to me." "Doesn't that piece down there, that is holding up the locking joint, look a bit weak? Like a thin milk bottle?" There were other comparisons to objects, especially to faces. "That lower part of the lip there." "The chin is weak." Between Henry Moore and Isaac Witkin there was immediate understanding. Moore's hand drew a quick stroke with a ball-point pen down a sheet of lined note paper, and Witkin assented, "Yes, yes." The eye not the mind appeared to do the judging. When he is making formal decisions, Moore's face loses its affable charm; his eyes brighten and his face becomes concentrated and intense. Sometimes Moore bounded up to the plaster itself, and taking a long stick pointed to a protuberance or a hollow, talking in little bursts. With his sporty checks and his long stick he looked like Don Quixote as a country gentleman.

"It's not easy. It's not easy," Henry Moore kept saying, between his corrections. When the big sculptures-in-process are outside all the time, in the summer, these conferences go on several times a day, and work goes faster than it does in the winter. "Sometimes you have to carry a curve really far out before you know that it's wrong: another part gets finished that changes things." Today the sun was bright and looked warm, but everyone was stamping his feet to keep his toes from freezing. Though it was not long past noon, the low winter sun cast the manlike shadow of the Glenkiln Cross across the grass. "This in here looks a little *too* round and that will make it narrower." By one o'clock, the Locking Piece had been shifted around on its small wheels until it returned to its original place. "Our shape isn't quite right here, in the face, in the nose here. It looks to me as if it should be a little bit wider at the bottom. The biggest width should be low down, not in the middle. That is, there would be more *weight* down here. Well, there we are. Let's call it a morning's work." The assistants decided to leave it outside, to begin work in the open air after lunch. It would take them three or four days to follow out the morning's directions.

Lunch was on the sun porch again, boiled gammon, potatoes and cabbage. Sheila cooked it, and her simple lunches are the Moores' main meal. Before Sheila came to work, the Moores sometimes lacked a main meal. If Irina was absorbed in gardening, Henry would suggest boiled eggs, or just cheese and crackers for lunch. Things are more regular now, with a hot meal at noon and a cold plate at night— perhaps potted shrimps or cold chicken or cheese or sliced beef. In London, where they eat at least once a week, the Moores often treat themselves to the Café Royal, a lavish restaurant on Regent Street near Piccadilly Circus.

Moore seemed pleased with the morning's work and chatted lightly among the women who surrounded him. He ate quickly, talking between bites, and when he finished his pudding, rested for a few minutes in the small, old living room at the front of the house. Since the addition of the new wing, this has become the telly room, and the Moores spend many evenings here watching "Coronation Street" and "Z Cars." In the daytime the room is cold and dark but relieved by a wood fire and the presence of works of art, primitives and Henry Moores. As Moore talked sleepily after lunch—a ten-minute talking nap—his hands idly caressed a bronze maquette, and moved to a pebble, and moved again to an old wooden stringed figure of his own.

Then abruptly he stood, stretched and strode out to the far room again, to work some more on his waxes. The room had warmed up to 60 degrees and the wax was more malleable. It was two o'clock, and he lit the fluorescent lamp in the ceiling of the small studio. Darkness would come on soon—in December in England—and now he would not notice its coming. With another strip of paper ignited at the electric fire, he started the alcohol lamp burning again, and set to work. For an hour there was no interruption. In the house Mrs. Tinsley typed letters and coped with the telephone. Outside the studio five hundred yards away Isaac Witkin and Ron Swan were adding and subtracting plaster from the Locking Piece. Moore worked over one wax and then another, finishing neither. Then there was a knock on the door; Mrs. Tinsley apologized, but the *New York Times* was calling from London, and absolutely insisted that she speak to him. "They want to know if they can photograph the Lincoln Center Reclining Figure." (Moore had stopped work on it temporarily, to finish the Locking Piece.)

"No."

"I told them I was sure they couldn't."

"Tell them it's in the agreement."

"They want to know how far along it is, and they want to interview you about it. They want to talk with you now."

Moore looked perplexed and irritated, not wanting to refuse and not wanting to interrupt his work. "Tell them I'm in a mix of plaster," he said, and returned to his waxes.

Another hour went by undisturbed. A wax was finished and put in the box with the two finished that morning. Then Mrs. Tinsley returned. Gordon Bunshaft was on the phone from New York. Bunshaft had consulted the owners of the Banque Lambert in Brussels, and was able to give Moore one extra week on the Locking Piece. Moore put down the phone elated; now he felt sure he could finish the piece and have it in Brussels on time. And now was a good moment to break for tea.

Tea was in the big dining room at the front of the house, where the Moores had breakfasted eight hours before. (By this hour the sun porch was gray with early evening.) Flowers filled the center of the table, and Irina poured tea for Henry and Mrs. Tinsley. There was a cake which Irina had bought at a church sale in Much Hadham, and a plate of cookies. The conversation picked up from lunch. Mary returned halfway through, and was quickly the center of attention. The phone rang in the office and Mrs. Tinsley left the table to answer it. A telegram from Australia requested the "world's greatest sculptor" to design a monument in Sydney. He would refuse it, but smiled happily at the phrase.

After tea Moore worked another half-hour on a wax, and put it away in the box with the others. The day counted four waxes finished, and a large step forward on the Locking Piece. Now he reluctantly turned off the lights and the heaters in the far room, locked the door and spent an hour dictating urgent letters. Then Mrs. Tinsley went home, and an old friend arrived from London to show Moore a 1932 drawing, a sketch for sculpture which the friend had bought at an auction. Moore remembered making the drawing, and the two of them talked about it while they had a drink in the new living room. The wing was added in 1960, a room and bath for Mary above it. The floor of the sunny living room is covered with a gold carpet, and against the walls are a variety of paintings and sculptures: a Cézanne cartoon for The Bathers, an explosive painting by Alan Davie, the figure of an angel from a Renaissance church, and in a niche near the ceiling three standing leaf figures by Henry Moore.

After half an hour Irina and Mary joined Moore and his old friend, and after another half-hour the friend left to return to London. For supper, on trays in front of the telly, the Moores moved back to the old living room, and watched television until 9:30, when Henry drove Mary to her dance. Since someone else was bringing her back, he went

19

Hoglands from the front

Irina on the sun porch

home to bed and slept. The huge white shape of the Locking Piece, altered since he saw it last, shimmered faintly in the glass-topped studio at the end of the garden.

It was not a typical day, but no day is typical. Sometimes he is in London all day, sitting on a committee, going to a show, visiting a bronze foundry. In summer he goes back and forth from old studios to new on a bicycle. On many days his afternoon is interrupted by visitors, whom he shows around with great courtesy, explaining things for the hundredth time without boredom. Visitors range from a single collector or art critic to busloads of students. Sometimes in the evening he will sketch, not drawing for exhibition but letting his pencil idly carry forms across the page, not knowing himself quite what will happen next. Other evenings, if the mood is on him, he will sit in the far room with a piece of clay and try to make a new shape, a shape that in a few months may rear in the ghost-white of plaster, in a big new studio at the bottom of the garden.

Weekends are a different routine. Saturday mornings are Irina's time out. The Moores drive to Bishop's Stortford late Saturday morning and do their shopping. At one o'clock they have lunch at the Foxley Hotel. They are home by 2:30 to receive the Saturday visitors. Sunday is spent at home in quiet, and Sunday morning now is usually Moore's best time for work. If the work doesn't go well, he feels awful: "I'm terribly sad, remembering childhood when we could have no pleasure on Sunday. It's a Puritan northern feeling, that Sunday feeling." But mostly he works well, and he looks forward to this morning all week. The boys are not there, there are no phone calls from architects or newspapers, there is no mail, no Mrs. Tinsley and no photographers. There is nothing but silent studios and the world of forms.

Moore put the final touches to his Locking Piece on Sunday morning, January 26, 1964. The assistants had done their last work the day before, and the plaster was painted a realistic bronze-color, but Moore enjoyed being alone with it, touching it, making little changes. Monday the 27th the truck came for it, one of those huge low-loaders, which usually carry heavy road equipment. A crane, built into a separate truck, lifted the sculpture onto the low-loader, and it started for Brussels. When it arrived the plaster had cracked and Isaac Witkin flew over to mend it. It was sited, admired and accepted by the owners of the Banque Lambert, and it departed for Berlin to be cast. (Moore's

Berlin founder has the proper equipment to cast big bronzes; he often uses English founders for smaller sculptures.) As the low-loader was crossing the border into West Germany, the drivers discovered that the Locking Piece was cracking badly again, and they refused to drive further. Agents from the founder arrived and packed the pieces into wooden cases, and when the dismembered parts arrived in West Berlin, it seemed impossible that anyone could put it together again. Isaac Witkin took another European journey, and reassembled the Locking Piece, putting it together like a three-dimensional jigsaw puzzle.

The bronze was exhibited first at the Documenta III Exhibition at

Assistants painting the Locking Piece

Kassel in the summer of 1964. A new plaster cast of it appeared at the Gulbenkian Exhibition at the Tate in London at the same time. The Documenta bronze arrived at the Banque Lambert in October, 1964, and was sited on a bronze base. In the meantime, The Hague bought a second bronze of the edition, and the process of casting began all over again. Since the moment of the bone joint and the moment of the locking flints, there have been thousands of decisions, leading to two bronze shapes on the continent of Europe.

2

1898–1918:
The Roll of Honour

CASTLEFORD SECONDARY SCHOOL
ROLL OF HONOUR

R·Fawbert·W·Y	L·Kassell·Y&L	E·Norman·R·E
H·N·Nicholson·W·Y	H·Holmes·R·E	P·Loftus
J·W·Turner·R·N·R	S·Thorpe·K·R·R	J·Nicholson·R·F·A
A·Braley·R·F·A	H·Anson·R·G·A	J·Fawcett·R·F·A
F·Lapworth·K·O·Y·L·I	H·C·Hartley·R·F·A	C·E·Burnill·A·S·C
J·W·Farquhar·5th Devns	T·L·Shepherd·R·G·A	G·W·Bickerdike·R·N
W·Laister·R·F·A	J·H·Parker·K·O·Y·L·I	J·Featherstone·R·N
O·Lodge·R·A·M·C	N·Gover·K·R·R	J·W·Thornburn·K·O·Y·L·I
F·Wilson·R·E	R·G·Walker·R·E	K·Gee·A·O·C
H·E·Winn·Gur·R·1/5th	H·Terry·K·O·Y·L·I	C·H·Bellwood·R·N
E·Featherstone·R·F·A	E·P·Wilson·R·E	H·S·Moore·C·S·R
W·Firth·W·Y	W·S·Firth·R·E	R·J·Holroyd·C·G
C·Brown·R·F·A	A·Smith·R·E	H·Firth
A·Hopkinson·A·S·C	I·Parker	J·E·Pearson·R·G·A
J·Stather·R·F·A	W·Waite·R·E	A·Morton·D·L·I
L·Monk·R·G·A	C·Hartley·R·F·A	B·E·Taylor·A·C·C
R·R·Soar·R·N·B	A·Parkin·A·S·C	A·Wright·W·Y
J·L·Martin·R·N·D	F·Gregory·S·H	A·Proctor·K·O·Y·L·I
G·Gregory·R·E	C·Appleyard·R·F·C	W·H·Smith·R·N·V·R
S·Gregory·R·E	D·Drake·Lincs	C·E·Bentley·W·Y
J·Walker·R·G·A	P·Robbins·A·S·C	A·Bleasby·S·S
E·Dean·R·E	J·H·Didlock·R·G·A	W·E·Hough·R·N
W·Tibbs·R·N·D	G·W·Blackburn	W·A·D·Lawson·W·R
F·Barton·W·Y	W·Varley·R·N	A·Wainwright·R·F·C
L·J·Castle·D·C·L·I	H·E·Fish	J·W·Woodcock·D·L·I
J·L·Rodger·A·S·C	C·Wheater	A·Dalby·R·N·V·R
H·Hartley·A·S·C	W·Bickerton	
R·R·Nicholson·R·F·A	E·Bagnall·R·N	
H·Balmforth·R·N	W·Barker	H·Wright
L·Veitch·R·G·A	H·Ogden	N·Grant
A·Chilton·K·O·Y·L·I	F·Woodcock	S·Gledhill

1914-19

THE Locking Piece and all its cousins in stone, wood and bronze had their origins in Castleford, Yorkshire, one hundred and fifty miles to the north. Like every other English town, Castleford has its memorials of the Great War; inside the entrance to the Grammar School hangs a Roll of Honour, which lists in gold paint, seventy-third of its ninety-one names of pupils who served in the First World War, "H–S–Moore–C–S–R" (Henry Spencer Moore, Civil Service Rifles). The scroll does not only list the name of the school's most distinguished alumnus; it is his first carving.

No one will claim that it anticipates his genius. It shows that he could do a job of work at the age of seventeen without any training at all. At the top of the scroll is the seal of the school and then the lettering:

Castleford   Secondary

School

ROLL   OF   HONOUR

To each side of the word "school" are ornamental oak leaves, projecting like the letters and seal from a cutaway background. At the bottom is the date "1914–19 " with the war's end a blank. Moore did the carving in 1916, the year before he went off to war himself; afterward, he never got around to adding the final digits. When the scroll was moved a few years ago, the present headmaster discovered on the back Moore's scratch sheet, his practice for the front. "A B C D," he starts, and then goes on more ambitiously: "DESIGNED AND EXECUTED BY H. S. MOORE." Underneath are more letters and initials, and a swift chisel sketch of Moore's own headmaster, complete with pince-nez, straw hat and mustache.

Moore was born in Castleford, a coal-mining town a few miles out of Leeds, July 30, 1898. Castleford is long rows of virtually identical attached low brick houses, with identical coal smoke dragging itself out of identical chimneys; the streets in movies like "Saturday Night and Sunday Morning" or "Room at the Top." Over the town hover slag heaps and the enormous winding wheels at the pit heads. When Moore was a child the chemical industry lagged behind coal, with glassmak-

ing a poor third. In the eighteenth century Castleford had been a pottery town—there are clay pits everywhere—and its Dunderdale Ware was exported to Spain and elsewhere on the Continent, but the Napoleonic Wars ruined the trade. There were no trees, no old buildings or handsome new ones, nothing for the eye to look at with pleasure. The landscape of the spirit was like the outward landscape; the word "mucky" was a common synonym for "dirty," and Moore remembers the proverb, "Where there's muck there's money." Industry was always present. "Our road led to Glasshoughton Colliery and very early in the morning, quite often, one would be wakened by the miners all tramping to work in their clogs. This might be at half-past four in the morning. In the wintertime this always sounded to me very strange and weird, coming up to a crescendo of clogs and then dying away."

Yet for a young child the landscape he knows has its own prodigies. "The slag heaps of Castleford in my youth were mountains," Moore remembers, and unconsciously praises the artificial by calling it natural. Moore wonders if the contrasts of industry and nature in his childhood are responsible for the organic form of his sculpture. Within a mile of where he grew up there were five coal mines, two chemical works, three coke ovens and some small potteries. During holidays from school he escaped the industrial city by walking out into the rough Yorkshire countryside, where he had friends whose fathers were farmers, and where he sometimes helped at harvest.

Henry Moore's father, Raymond, was a coal miner whose grandfather had come over from Ireland. Raymond started work on a farm when he was nine, and later came to Castleford to go down into the pits. He was an ambitious man. With almost no official schooling he conducted his education in private. He read all of Shakespeare, and taught himself mathematics and engineering until he passed examinations to become qualified as a mine manager. Then a pit accident damaged his eyesight, and he couldn't advance to the higher position. His ambition turned entirely to his children. He did not like being a coal miner, and he saw to it that none of his children ever knelt at a coal face. Still, some art critics have made much of the fact that Henry Moore's father's work involved cutting rock.

Henry was the seventh of eight children, and his father was fifty and his mother forty when he was born. He was the youngest son, and a sister two years younger died when he was fifteen, leaving him the youngest child. "I got the best of it, of course." His father provided an education, on his small salary, for each of the children. The eldest son, also Raymond, went to work as a schoolteacher when Henry was eleven, and contributed to the family income. This allowed the Moores to move from 30 Roundhill Road (where Henry was born) a block away to a slightly larger house, 65 Smawthorne Lane, across from a late nineteenth-century decorative pub. Young Raymond and his sister Mary, who was also a schoolteacher, became schoolmasters when they were still young. Willie died before Henry was born, Annie married a glassworker, Betty a schoolteacher, and only Alfred remained unaccounted for: He emigrated to Canada and was never heard from again.

The father's strength and ambition were the force behind this family. His crowded working-class house was more intellectual and artistic than the houses of the Castleford middle class. There were books and gramophone records, and there were also political convictions. When Henry was less than ten, Raymond Moore took part in a strike that lasted two years; to make enough money to feed their children, Raymond became a shoemaker and Mary a laundress. Raymond was an early trades-unionist. One president of the Miners' Federation, Herbert Smith, drank tea in the parlor, the site also of early meetings of the Labor party. Socialism in the elder Raymond Moore's mind was not to be distinguished from social mobility. It was still the age of *Smile's Self Help.*

Henry Moore's memory of his father is a bit fearful. Such energy—so thwarted in its own goals—created an authoritarian "complete Victorian father, aloof, spoiled like all of them in those days." Moore remembers, "No one could sit in his particular chair." When Henry failed the scholarship to the Secondary School the first time he sat for it, his father forced him to take it again. He would have stopped going to school if his father had not pushed him. Later when he wanted to go to art school, his father insisted that he qualify as a teacher first, like his brother and sister.

His father is the source of the family's ambition and energy, but his mother is ultimately more responsible for the kind of artist Moore became. Whenever he models a reclining figure or a mother with child (almost all his sculpture is of women), he is reaching back to Mary Moore. If he feared his aloof father, he loved his mother's female presence. "I suppose I've got a mother complex," he says, without letting it worry him. Mary Moore was "absolutely feminine, womanly, motherly." When he was a small child and she left the house he cried until she returned. He remembers how hard she had to work: At 4:30 in the morning she helped ready her husband for the morning shift at the pit, and she kept busy with children and cooking and washing and housework until late at night. He never saw her rest. Sometimes she had a pain in her shoulder, and she let him rub it for her; when he was nearly sixty, and working on the plaster of a large figure of a pregnant woman, he thought continually of rubbing his mother's back. "I could almost have made it without looking at it. The sense of touch, the boniness across the backbone."

She was a humorous woman, affectionate and vain. Moore's friend Raymond Coxon painted her portrait in London in 1925, when she was a widow (Raymond Moore died in 1922). She was no longer young, but she kept comparing herself to the portrait of a young girl which hung in Coxon's studio. "Couldn't I have a long neck?" she would say. She sat for her portrait in a rocking chair, and sawed back and forth so vigorously that at one point she rocked herself head over heels. Coxon called, "Keep your head up, Sparrow!" and she was undamaged.

Mary Moore lived with one of her daughters, or in a cottage near

Raymond Coxon's portrait
of Moore's mother

Moore's sketch of his mother

Henry Moore's mother

one of them, until she died in 1944 at eighty-four. She visited Henry and Irina in London, Kent and Hertfordshire. During one visit to London, she spent a day outside, rugged up in a chair, while Henry carved a block of stone. At lunch time he was covered with stone dust, and when he put down his tools and came to unpack her, she looked at him and sighed, thinking of her other children in clean schoolrooms, "Ee, Henry lad, why did you ever take it up?"

He took it up—deciding to be a great sculptor—when he was ten. "Our Sunday School teacher told us how, when Michelangelo was carving his Head of a Faun, someone said, 'But that's an old faun; surely an old faun would have lost some of its teeth?' Michelangelo took up his chisel and knocked two of the teeth out. 'There you are,' our teacher said. 'There's the greatest sculptor in the world ready to take advice.' What went click in my mind was not the moral but the fact that this was the greatest sculptor who ever lived. I'd always liked our drawing classes, and I'd carved bits of wood and stone. Now, instead of saying I wanted to be an engine-driver, I said I wanted to be a sculptor." He is still competing with Michelangelo.

Some early modeling and carving, long before the extant Roll of Honour, happened with children's games. The boys from his Temple Street School played in clay pits sometimes—there was one two hundred yards from his house—by making "touchwood ovens," which were little clay boxes about four inches square, with a hole at one end and another on top. They put wood from a dead tree inside the box and lighted it with a match. By blowing through the hole in the side you could get a bright glow from the box, and keep your hands warm in winter. Sometimes they made decorations on the sides of the touchwood ovens, little clay reliefs. Sometimes the hole on top would turn into a chimney, and the chimney look like a man. Then there was a game called "piggy," which involved carving a piece of wood into a particular shape so that it jumped into the air when you hit it with a stick.

The Secondary School, which Moore entered when he was twelve, was founded only in 1906, and the main building—a late flower of Victorian decoration, with façades a little like Cycladic violin figures—opened in 1909, a year before Moore matriculated. In 1910 it was not common for a working-class child to attend school after the age of twelve. Miners traditionally cared more for education than factory workers or farmhands, but often the family could not afford to let a boy stay out of work. The rich sent their children to boarding school, and the grammar schools existed for the children of shopkeepers and small managers.

The headmaster whom Moore caricatured, T. R. Dawes, was an unusual man, "decades ahead of his time" to Moore, who remembers him with affection and some amusement. An evangelist of wit and intellect, he was forever coaxing visiting lecturers and performers into his school. Once after a concert he was delighted to hear Henry Moore, the coal miner's son, whistling some Mozart. "Do that again!" he said, charmed at his success in promoting good music. Moore didn't tell him that his father was continually playing the same piece on their gramophone. Another of Dawes' passions was English Church architecture, and he often took pupils on excursions to the best examples in villages outside Castleford. He had them learn "Never Eat Dirty Potatoes" to remember the order of the styles: Norman, Early English, Decorative and Perpendicular.

It was perhaps Dawes who introduced Moore to Methley Church (Methley is a village a couple of miles from Castleford), which Moore has always named as one of the sources of his sculpture, or at least of his early absorption with direct carving. The carvings in Methley Church were almost the only sculpture he saw before he went to the Leeds School of Art in 1919. They are strong old Gothic heads, distorted and expressive, without decoration or detail. Moore drew them, for his own pleasure, when he was very young. Inside the church there are touching catafalques, dogs crouched under the feet of medieval ladies and gentlemen who are delicately and accurately represented in death. Moore does not even remember them.

The most important person in his life at this time was not T. R. Dawes but Miss Alice Gostick. In his first year at the Secondary School, Moore had an art teacher who objected to the figures in his drawings; their feet hung down like tassels, she said. Moore didn't like that. But in 1911 Miss Gostick, who appreciated him, took over the art classes. She lived in town with her mother, who was French and a pianist who gave recitals at the school. Miss Gostick and her mother brought to Castleford an intimation of the world of art. She had what seemed to her students the artist's temperament, gentle and generous. She invited her best pupils to her house for tea every Sunday, and showed them magazines like *Studio* and *Colour,* which illustrated new art. Her house was the only place in Castleford where one could begin to know what

A head from Methley Church

was happening, or had happened not long ago, in Paris. For Moore, from thirteen to eighteen, she was representative of the life he dreamed of attaining.

Her three best pupils were Arthur Dalby, Albert Wainwright and Henry Moore. When there was anything artistic to do for the school—like designing a poster, or the cover for a theatrical program, or sets for the play, or carving the Roll of Honour—these three boys were the candidates and Miss Gostick chose the lucky one. The most sensational of her students at this time was not Henry Moore but Albert Wainwright, who was sophisticated enough to be influenced, mostly by Aubrey Beardsley. (He continued his artistic career by designing for the theater at Leeds until he died suddenly at the age of 40. Arthur Dalby, who died in 1960, inspected art schools for the Ministry of Education.) All of them were indebted and grateful to Miss Gostick. Moore corresponded with her regularly until she died at eighty-seven in the spring of 1964. She had written not long before to congratulate him on his election to the Order of Merit.

Most of the art work in school was drawing, but Moore persisted in his ambition to become a sculptor like Michelangelo. When the school decided it should have a Roll of Honour, Miss Gostick chose Moore to do the carving, and lent him her own wood-carving tools. It was the first time he had ever carved with proper equipment, and though he had no illusions about what he was doing, he was excited to dig into the oak and carve a public shape.

Moore's birthplace

Moore at age eleven

Moore as a soldier

Moore was not extraordinary outside of art class. He played games and took part in plays and was slightly above average in his other subjects. In his last year, when he was eighteen, Moore did practice teaching in his old elementary school. If the war had not interrupted him, he would have spent two years at a training college and become a schoolteacher like his brother and sister. He joined the Civil Service Rifles (15th London Regiment) in February, 1917. He went off to training camp and in Castleford someone painted "H–S–Moore–C–S–R" on the scroll he had carved. He was young, silly and intent on coming home a hero covered with medals. He went to the front in the summer of 1917, and was soon in the thick of it. "Sometimes in France there were three or four days of great danger when you thought there wasn't a chance of getting through, and then all one felt was sadness for having taken so much trouble to no purpose." But he was young enough, and was back home soon enough, so that he can say without irony, "On the whole I enjoyed the army."

The height, and finale of his career at the front was the Battle of Cambrai, in November and December, 1917. Moore was a member of a Lewis Gun team, the one who held the gun and fired it. On November 20 the English mounted the first great tank attack. Moore's company followed the tanks through the German lines, and when the Germans counterattacked ten days later, they dug into a hillock at the edge of a green field. On the fourth day they were still there—the ones who were alive—and could not see a blade of grass before them.

When German planes began to strafe his company, Moore asked permission of an officer to shoot back at them with his Lewis Gun. "No, no!" the officer told him. "It would only attract attention and get us strafed all the more!" Moore then asked if he could take the gun a hundred yards away and do it: "I was daftest." Moore's Lewis Gun squad—a Corporal in charge—was to occupy a shell hole in front of their lines and shoot at German airplanes. "It was like trying to hit a particular brick in a house, with the house going past you at eighty miles an hour." In the shell hole the Lewis Gun team found a bottle of rum miraculously intact. They each had a tot, and then the Corporal had another and another. Finally, "I sat on the bottle to keep him from getting drunk," and the Battle of Cambrai spent itself while Henry Moore sat on a bottle of rum in a shell hole in no man's land firing at airplanes. Later the Corporal was given a medal.

Of the four hundred men in his regiment, Moore was one of fifty-two who were able to muster on the last day when the battle was over. Of those fifty-two, the voices of twenty-five were affected by gas, and they were sent to the hospital. Moore was one. (Their gas masks were primitive and uncomfortable. They sniffed the gas a bit before they put their masks on, and took a few sniffs later to see if the coast was clear. Sometimes it wasn't, and over four days of gassing they inhaled quite a bit even though they were careful.) The twenty-five marched with painful lungs ten miles to the hospital. After three months' recuperating in England, Moore was fit to become cadre, and spent the last months of the war teaching recruits the use of the bayonet.

When he was discharged he returned to Castleford, and Miss Gostick performed one more supremely important act of service. She arranged an Ex-Serviceman's Grant—a Great War anticipation of the G.I. Bill of Rights—that would pay for Moore to attend Leeds School of Art. His father didn't like the idea; but "by now I had been two years away from home, and felt more grown up, and was determined to do what *I* wanted." With the aid of the worst war in history, he had broken out of the circle of Castleford and schoolteaching, and the world of art lay ahead of him.

In Miss Gostick's garden,
after the War

3

1919–1924:
The Renaissance Head

HENRY Moore arrived at Leeds School of Art as an elderly student of twenty-one. Barbara Hepworth came up a year later at the age of sixteen, which was more typical. He worked extremely hard, he thinks because he was so relieved not to be dead. As Moore the soldier had wanted to be the bravest, now he was trying to sketch as well as Leonardo. He and his best friend Raymond Coxon thought and talked art all day long, and tried to make use of every moment. As they walked to class they might watch—trying to understand spatially and memorize—the movement of a horse's haunches as it pulled a load uphill. By four in the afternoon, they were too discouraged to speak, so huge was the discrepancy between the morning's ambitions and the day's accomplishments. They drank their tea in silence.

Moore lived in Castleford to save money and commuted five or six days a week. He went up to Leeds on the 8:10, which meant rising early because the station was half an hour's walk from his house. Leeds is only ten miles from Castleford, but he took the early train so that he could get a good seat for the 9:30 life-drawing class. After the 2:30 class, and tea, he and Coxon worked in the reference library until evening classes, which ended at nine. Moore caught the 9:25 at Leeds Station, waited to change at Lofthouse, got to Castleford at 10:20 and was home by 10:50. Then he ate a small supper and did his homework —perhaps anatomy or perspective—until one o'clock.

He was more disciplined, harder working and a little bit better at all his subjects than his fellow students. No Albert Wainwright outshone him now. The first year was all drawing and painting, and the life drawing brought out Moore's instinct for monumentality. But sketching plaster casts disturbed him, because it gave him doubts about his old desire to be a sculptor. He disliked the casts, and thought that there was something wrong with him. Then he found that they were poor pieces in themselves—late Roman copies of Greek originals—and that they had been whitewashed every year for twenty years. They staggered under a quarter of an inch of whitewash, which blurred whatever distinction the forms might have had. These *bad* examples of classical sculpture, Moore thinks, encouraged him to look elsewhere for a sculptural tradition.

41

Moore's program cover

Moore talking with Miss Gostick;
Raymond Coxon behind

The teaching at Leeds was no better than the plaster casts. One professor advised his better pupils to go to London as soon as possible, and that was the best teaching they had. But in the meantime Moore was curious, and he was making discoveries for himself. The library was useful; the collector Sir Michael Sadler opened his house to art students, and showed them their first post-impressionists. At the end of the year Moore passed his exams predictably. But earlier, he and Raymond Coxon had won greater glory. Leeds had prize competitions in a variety of categories; Moore and Coxon applied themselves diligently to all of them. On prize day when the awards were granted they had taken every one. Among Henry Moore's was the prize for fashion design.

At vacations and on weekends he kept up with things in Castleford. (He had taught at an elementary school there, between mustering out and matriculating at Leeds.) He took Raymond Coxon home with him, to meet Miss Gostick and Arthur Dalby, and they turned some jugs together on the Secondary School pottery wheel. Groups of Miss Gostick's pupils, old and new, gathered to paint designs on pottery as well. Moore joined the Old Boys Association, in which he played soccer and tennis. He and his partners won the doubles and mixed doubles tournaments in 1919. In 1920 he wrote, produced and starred in his verse play, *Narayana and Bhataryan*—influenced by the exotic orientalism of James Elroy Flecker, and "Dedicated to the Memory of Rupert Brooke." He had been writing poems all along, though none has survived; if both his arms had been shot off in the war, he had thought at the time, he would have tried to be a writer. No known copy of the play exists, but some of the cast remember lines, like, "Kandisata must have her sacrifice tonight!" (Kandisata was a hippopotamus-goddess; Moore made up all the names.) One actor was required to inspect an obvious corpse, turn to the audience and announce: "Dead!" as portentously as possible.

Later the play was performed a second time, as the first-year students' show at the Royal College of Art in London. It was not a great success. Moore stopped writing, but unlike many artists he did a lot of reading—novels mostly. He had spells of the Russians, Tolstoy and Dostoevsky in particular, then a spell of Hardy or of Stendhal. One of his strongest admirations was for D. H. Lawrence, which is as it should be: Both men are working-class sons of coal miners, strongly attached to their mothers; both are powerfully emotional artists, attracted to the primitive; both are intensely English and both (for different reasons and in different ways) had trouble with the English public. Yet for all the sexuality of Moore's reclining figures and Lawrence's novels, the men are opposites in character: Moore is gentle, accommodating and vigorously concentrated on artistic form; Lawrence was violent, intractable and anti-formalist.

In his second and final year at Leeds, Moore had the advantage of a Department of Sculpture that consisted of a single instructor who had lately graduated from the Royal College of Art. (Leeds started a new department because one student wanted it, and the student turned out to be Henry Moore.) The instructor concentrated on teaching Moore all the tricks he had learned, and Moore was able to squeeze a two-year examination course into one year and win a scholarship to the

Jug painted by Moore in Castleford

Royal College of Art as well. His academic training was in conventional representational modeling, and he was good at it. For the examination he modeled a hand, which was later sent to other English art schools as an example of how the thing should be done.

Probably the most important event at Leeds for Moore's artistic development was reading a book which he found in the Leeds City Public Library, Roger Fry's *Vision and Design*. It was here, in the argument and in the illustrations, that Moore first encountered primitive sculpture. (The Gothic heads at Methley Church have similar strong sculptural feeling, but they are not primitive.) Fry dealt in particular with African Negro sculpture, and emphasized the three-dimensional quality of it and its truth to material. Both ideas became principles to Henry Moore.

Moore was by no means the first artist to learn from the primitive.

There was Gauguin years before—and Brancusi and Modigliani and Picasso and Lipchitz and Derain—and Epstein close at hand. But along with Derain and Epstein he was among the first to study the subject thoroughly, to the point where he became an inadvertent scholar of ancient sculpture. Primitivism as a romantic idea had existed for a hundred and fifty years, but it was not until recently that it had become a sculptural force. Epstein says in his *Autobiography* that when he was a young man in New York "no one thought of Mexican or pre-Columbian Indian art"; instead, he wanted to go to Europe to see the monuments of Renaissance sculpture. For Moore a few years later, Europe was London, and *Vision and Design* led Moore not to the Renaissance but to the Ethnographical Gallery of the British Museum.

The British Museum has been the most salient source of all his sculpture. Stocked with the loot of empire, it contains carvings from all places and ages. Best known is Lord Elgin's famous haul from the Acropolis, but the Elgin marbles meant little to Moore at first; what moved him were the monuments of earlier civilizations like Egypt and Sumeria, and of alien cultures like Mexico and Africa, Polynesia and the Cyclades. In an article written a decade later, Moore declared that "a hundred years or so of Greece no longer blot our eyes to the sculptural achievements of the rest of mankind. Paleolithic and Neolithic sculpture, Sumerian, Babylonian and Egyptian, Early Greek, Chinese, Etruscan, Indian, Mayan, Mexican and Peruvian, Romanesque, Byzantine and Gothic, Negro, South Sea Island and North American Indian. . ." There is a breathlessness about his list which he has never lost. He daydreams still of making exhibitions of British Museum material. He would like to assemble pieces "*so* alike, and yet which couldn't have influenced each other. It would show there's a fundamental sculptural *thing*." One English scholar has said that Moore is probably the only single person who knows what's *in* the British Museum.

For years these examples of sculptures had been on view to anyone who cared to look at them, but virtually no one had been able to look at them as works of art. "I went to the British Museum on Wednesday and Sunday afternoons," says Moore, and a new ideal of "virility and power" replaced "beauty . . . the realistic ideal of physical beauty in art which sprang from fifth-century Greece was only a digression from

Cycladic sculpture

Cycladic sculpture

English pot

Mexican figure

the main world tradition of sculpture." He loved, as opposed to the Classical, "the Archaic Greek room with its life-size female figures, seated in easy, still naturalness, grand and full like Handel's music."

Now he began to explore other museums too, and studied Gothic sculpture at the Victoria and Albert. London was "a most tremendous exhilaration. For the first year I was in a dream of excitement. When I rode on the open top of a bus I felt that I was traveling in Heaven, almost, and that the bus was floating in the air. And it was Heaven all over again in the evenings, in my horrid little room in Sydney Street, where I could spread out the books I'd got out of the library and know that I had the chance of learning about all the sculptures that had ever been made in the world."

Domestic life began badly in the "horrid little room" he mentions, where the door struck the bed as soon as you opened it, and the landlady served wretched, dry finnan haddock every morning. ("She must have bought a carload of it cheap.") After one term there he moved in with Raymond Coxon, who had also moved to the Royal College, in a room in South Kensington. They worked together much of the day, and when they went to bed they were still talking, about "God, women and fine art." It was a small room, on Seymour Place, at twenty-two shillings a week. Among their elders at the College, they had the reputation of being wild, based on a few parties and a string of girls. But they were remarkably innocent. Looking back on it, Coxon remembers the Army accusation of innocence, "You can't say shit." "That was true," he says. "Henry couldn't say shit."

They kept track of time by separating it into sections named after

Moore and Coxon
in Castleford

the food they were eating. There was the Black Pudding Period, when they bought black puddings for breakfast every morning. There was the Baked Beans Period, when they bought an immense hoard of baked beans at twopence halfpenny a can—war surplus baked beans, salvaged from a sunken ship. An imitation Leonardo drawing by Henry Moore, *echt* Baked Beans Period, hangs now on Raymond Coxon's wall. They worked as intensely as they had worked in Leeds, and with growing confidence and freedom. Sometimes they would paint and carve all night. One would suggest to the other, in a casual way, "How about an all-night sitting tonight?" (The phrase "all-night sitting" derives from a Parliamentary habit.) The other, not to be outdared, would have to agree. Coxon always got sleepy first; Moore kept at it until about seven o'clock.

From Kensington, Moore and Coxon moved to an unfurnished flat in Walham Green that they rented for ten shillings and sixpence a week (about $2.50 then). They furnished the flat out of junk shops. Later still they moved to a real studio on Adie Road. They were not the best housekeepers, wherever they were. They kept forgetting to send the laundry, and sometimes Moore wore a dirty shirt inside out because he didn't have a clean one. The dishes they piled in the bath and only washed once a week. When he washed dishes, as when he carved, Moore sang at the top of his lungs. An old friend reports that he sounded like a coal man shouting, "Coal!" Mostly he sang "The Beggar's Opera" and Methodist hymns: "Till we meet at Jesu's seat," "Dare to be a Daniel, dare to stand alone" and "Crown Him Lord of all."

When they invited other students to their flat or studio, the Royal College knew about it. "There would be parties," says one old friend, "until five in the morning. They put potatoes in the jerry, and the polite girls said it was about time to go." (A jerry is a chamber pot.) Both at Leeds and the Royal College of Art, Moore stood out for his exuberance as well as for his talent. "It was the Irish in him," says Coxon, "that made him stand out." For another party Moore made a drawing of five nudes, all of them party-goers. (Stephen Spender owns it now.) Coxon is in the middle looking Greek, and Moore to one side modestly turned about. Another man and two girls line up in a row, all undressed, but the effect is more of a prank than of a quintuple orgy. There was also a famous Party to Test the Influence of Drink on Work.

49

Moore and Coxon covered their walls with blank paper and made a list of subjects sacred and profane. Each participant had a drink, drew a rectangle, numbered it, and drew a picture. Then he had a second drink and drew a second picture. Investigation the next day determined that most artists improved steadily through the fifth drink, and then deteriorated rapidly.

Meanwhile there was the four-year course at the Royal College of Art. Moore was quickly accepted as a leader among the students. Sir John Rothenstein—whose father Sir William was principal of the College—remembers meeting him the first time, and enjoying the talk without knowing his name. When Moore left, Rothenstein asked his sister, a student at the Royal College of Art, who the young man was. "He's going to be a great sculptor," she said. The teachers were not convinced. Leon Underwood was a help to him, especially in drawing, but the others required ignoring and outwitting. At the monthly session when each student submitted a drawing for public criticism by the professors, Moore ran into difficulties; once some trees he had drawn were "shockingly Cézannesque"; another time a teacher declared, "This student has been feeding on garbage." Moore remembers that the piece was slightly Etruscan.

It was a time for being influenced, though not by one's professors. In his first years at the college, Moore read Wyndham Lewis's *Blast*—which had come out while Moore was still in secondary school—with its denunciations of academic art and its promulgation of vorticism. The vorticist emphasis on will, on the self-created power of the artist, was agreeable to Moore, and so was Wyndham Lewis's advocacy of direct carving in stone, and his hatred of traditional modeling in clay or plaster. Also at this time Moore read Ezra Pound's *Gaudier-Brzeska*, his chaotic and affectionate memoir of the young vorticist sculptor who had been killed in France at the age of twenty-four. Pound also advocated carving, and printed photographs of Henri Gaudier-Brzeska's work—sometimes more cubist and static, sometimes more futurist and dynamic—and reprinted Gaudier's spirited essay on sculpture from *Blast*. In Gaudier, Moore found someone who agreed with him—praising primitive sculpture, *Blast*ing the Greeks and making strong slogans: "Sculptural energy is the mountain. Sculptural feeling is the appreciation of masses in relation. Sculptural ability is the defining of these masses by planes." In the Seymour Place studio Moore cut in plaster a

Moore in Yorkshire
about 1920

dancing figure whose legs are contorted like a frog's; she is in the act of jumping. The line of influence goes back through *Blast* and Gaudier to the great Italian futurist innovator, Umberto Boccioni.

Moore's knowledge of other modern sculptors was small at this time, partly because England was such an artistic backwater, and partly because the leaders of modern sculpture were still obscure even on the Continent. In England there were three sculptors who anticipated him in a small way. Frank Dobson carried the influence of Maillol to London, a livelier tradition than anything locally available. Eric Gill was a fanatic for carving, but his sculpture is affected and decorative. Jacob Epstein's primitivist work is not his best; he was really a portrait sculptor, and had already modeled in 1915 his great bronze bust of Admiral Lord Fisher. Though Epstein bought early Moores and was generous in a hundred ways, he was not an artistic mentor.

Among dealers, collectors and cognoscenti all over the world, sculpture was despised as a second-rate art. The *New Statesman* published an article saying that sculpture was dead and that architecture was the solid art of the future. It angered Moore at the time, but now he feels that the neglect into which sculpture had fallen left him free. "I'm glad there wasn't a sculptural tradition, that I had to learn it all from the British Museum, that sculpture was looked on as a dead art." Though Brancusi had been carving for some time in his Paris studio, and Archipenko and Lipchitz and Arp were already producing mature work, Moore's teachers were anonymous Toltecs and Congolese.

He was free in himself, at least; he was not free of the rules of academicians. At the Royal College there were so few sculpture students that Moore had a studio all to himself, but he was restricted in his use of it. In accordance with academic tradition, he was not supposed to do direct carving. Though his primitive mentors carved, and though to the avant-garde modeling was Philistine and distasteful, Moore was required to model in clay and then transfer the clay into stone by mechanical means. It was the tradition of Western sculpture. Even Rodin's marbles, for the most part, and most Renaissance sculptures, were executed by stone carvers using pointing machines to copy the sculptor's model. A pointing machine is a framework which is attached firmly to the clay model and to the block of stone. The carver measures exact distances from the outside of the frame to the model, and transfers this exact distance by boring a little hole into the stone, to

Mother and Child, 1922

a depth equal to the point in the clay model. The executed carving has tiny pores in it, which reveal that a pointing machine has been used.

Moore believed in carving and in truth to material; whatever was really stone should look stony, and wood woody. Therefore the idea of *modeling* something which was going to be *stone* was anathema. Also he believed in Michelangelo's old distinction: Sculpture is the art of cutting away, painting of building up from nothing. Therefore the modeler was really more painterly than sculptural. So when, in 1923, his professor at the Royal College required that he copy a Renaissance head from a plaster model into stone, Moore requested permission to carve it directly in marble. Permission was denied; Moore was to use a pointing machine for the carving, because otherwise he was certain to botch the job; no one could carve an accurate copy direct in stone.

Moore convinced his own instructor (who would see him at work; the professor would not) to let him have a go at carving it direct. The result stands in Raymond Coxon's house. It is a gracefully executed, conventionally beautiful Renaissance head, twenty-one inches high, and for Moore it serves to show the doubters that he *could* do old-fashioned pretty things if he *wanted* to. Its full title is Copy of the Head of the Virgin, and Moore copied it from the marble relief of the Virgin and Child by Domenico Rosselli in the Victoria and Albert Museum. Some critics, at least, find the Moore an improvement on the Rosselli. The Virgin's face turns out, at a slight angle, from a background relief, and the marble represents flesh as elegantly as the marble of any Court sculptor. It went against everything that Moore believed, except that he managed to carve it direct. The marble of the Virgin's face is delicately pored with small holes which Moore added when he had finished the carving, so that it would look as if he had used the pointing machine. The professor of sculpture was pleased.

Academic training aside, the Royal College was valuable to Moore, especially in the person of its principal. Sir William brought his brother Charles Rutherston (who had changed his name a few years earlier to sound less German) to visit Moore's studio, and Rutherston became the first collector to buy a Henry Moore carving; Moore cannot remember the price, but guesses that it might have been ten pounds. Rutherston also bought Coxon's portrait of Moore, which hangs in the Manchester City Art Gallery now. Later in the decade, he introduced

Detail from Masaccio's
Adam and Eve

Raymond Coxon's portrait
of Moore, 1924

Moore to Dorothy Warren whose London gallery gave Moore his first one-man show. Sir William entertained his students on Sunday nights, when they met poets and artists (Rabindranath Tagore, Ralph Hodgson, Walter de la Mare, Eric Gill) and even prime ministers (Ramsay MacDonald).

Then in 1924 Moore won a Royal College of Art Travelling Scholarship for a six-month visit to Italy. The scholarship came at a time when he was at his most dogmatically primitive and anticlassical; he had no desire to do another Renaissance head. He admired Michelangelo, but he feared giving in to him. He asked the Royal College if he couldn't spend the six months in Paris instead (Moore liked to go there every spring), but the authorities insisted that he stick to the terms of the scholarship, which specified Italy.

At first his dogmatism appeared unshaken. He wrote his principal the letter of a twenty-five-year-old to his patron. Excepting Michelangelo from the general censure, he lectured: "Giotto's painting is the finest sculpture I have met in Italy. . . . In the influence of Donatello I think I see the beginning of the end—Donatello was a modeler, and it seems to me that it is modeling that has sapped the manhood out of Western sculpture." He deplored "the widespread avoidance of thinking and working in stone." He foreshadowed: "The only hope I can see for a school of sculpture in England, under our present system, is a good artist working, carving in the big tradition of sculpture, who can get the sympathy and admiration of students. . . ."

When he wrote the letter he was most impressed by Giotto, but soon it was Masaccio who astonished him, and Masaccio has remained one of his great artistic influences. Moore spent half an hour every day at the Brancacci Chapel in the Church of Santa Maria del Carmine in Florence, where Masaccio grouped realistic, highly three-dimensional forms in fresco on a wall. Michelangelo had been there before him, as he knew; Vasari had written, "All the most celebrated sculptors since Masaccio's day have become excellent and illustrious by studying their art in this chapel." But for him, the immediate effect of Italy was interior chaos. He had to admit the validity of Renaissance "beauty," and the bravado of his letter to Sir William Rothenstein disappeared. He found it difficult to work, for almost the only time in his life. The lady whose Renaissance head Moore had faked so gracefully took her revenge upon him.

4

1925–1932:
The Leeds
Reclining Figure

W HEN Moore returned from Italy and finished his third year at the Royal College of Art, he was appointed instructor in the sculpture school for a term of seven years. He felt incredibly lucky in his job. For working two days a week (he never taught any more than that) he had a guaranteed income of 240 pounds ($1,200), which was enough to live on. And he could sell a few pieces of sculpture besides. Taking vacations into account he figured that he spent only 62 days a year at school, which left him 303 for work, 304 in Leap Year. "I couldn't have dreamed of better conditions. . . . I never thought that I couldn't do as well at sculpture as I should have done because I did that two days' teaching."

At the beginning, he thinks, the teaching even helped: "The first two or three years of teaching your own subject is as much a way of learning for the teachers as for the students themselves. I remember I used to be very surprised quite often at the things I discovered while teaching, the actual sentences, the words . . . after a few years of teaching then I think it isn't a very good thing, because there comes a stage when you have to repeat things that you think are fundamental in the training of a sculptor. They become a deadening thing." Teaching was onerous long before he quit, in fact, but most artists have to give up some of their time to earn their keep. While Henry Moore was teaching, Barbara Hepworth and Ben Nicholson were spending an equivalent amount of time doing posters and other commercial work.

Meanwhile the sculpture resumed, following the unsettling interruption of the Renaissance influence. Moore went back to the British Museum, and his fascination with the primitive reasserted itself. Now in a German book, one of the *Orbis Pictus* series, he found an illustration of an ancient limestone reclining figure, a representation of the Mayan rain spirit, Chac Mool, which had been found near Chichén Itzá in Mexico. He was ready to learn from Chac Mool—and was struck by its power and truth to material—but he was not yet ready to assimilate Masaccio. He coped with the Renaissance by refusing to let it touch his work.

Now also he discovered the Museum of Natural History, where he found another major source of his forms in the study of natural structures: cellular, skeletal, mineral. He brooded over skeletons, and became the world's foremost collector of pebbles. Until the Museum of Natural History intervened, the source of most of Moore's work had been art rather than nature. Probably the major source of most good art is other art, for that matter. Moore shows traces in his work of primitive art especially, but also of Picasso, Arp and Lipchitz: These artists show in their work traces of artists they learned from. (The Manhattan dealer who gave her opinion of Moore by saying, "Arp got there first. Who's better?" can be answered in two different ways. In the first place Brancusi got there before Arp. But more seriously, what does the primacy matter? Marlowe got there first but Shakespeare is better.) But sometimes an imitation is *too* close to the original, and the work of art suffers by being co-authored. Sir John Rothenstein prefers Moore's early drawings to his early carvings, because the carvings are derivative. "Were *Mask* of 1924 . . . placed with others in a collection of ancient Mexican sculpture, it would take an experienced scholar to pick it out as a modern derivation. Who, on the other hand, having ever seen one of the early drawings of seated women, could fail to attribute it . . . ?"

Roger Fry—the critic whose *Vision and Design* led Moore toward primitive art—once derided Moore by saying that Moore knew what

Chac Mool

works of art looked like, and so he tried to make them. Fry was not charging eclecticism so much as faking, a quality of the *voulu*. Looking at Moore's earliest work, one can see the source of the judgment, though one understands by this time how the immature carvings prepared the way to the great ones. Early pseudo-African pieces like the 1922 Head of a Girl are acts of homage more than of imagination. They are copies nearly as much as the Renaissance head, only in an alien tradition; they express technical skill, critical discrimination and a lack of artistic confidence. During the same years, Moore's life drawings were vital and individual, copies of nothing. When the primitive vigor of his carving united with the human sensuality of his life drawing, at the end of the twenties, Moore came into his prime as a sculptor. By that time the natural but inhuman forms of pebbles and skeletons and crystals had suggested new ways of dealing with the human form, ways which were not copied from primitive sculpture although they had its energy and coherence. When Moore copied distortions from the primitives, he imitated superstitious primitive feelings which were not his own. Theology, whether pagan or Christian, creates fearful or protective deities and spiritualized human images. Moore needed to distort through the organic forms of pebbles and trees in order to make his own statement.

Drawing remained highly important to him for many years. His graphic work until 1940 falls into two groups: life drawings of nudes and abstract ideas for sculpture. The latter were "a means of generating ideas for sculpture," he said, and "of sorting out ideas and developing them." On the other hand, life drawing "keeps one fit—like physical exercises—perhaps acts like water to a plant. . . . It enlarges one's form repertoire, one's form experience." Moore's naked women were part of his research into nature, like his study of pebbles and bones; they were also part of his theme of the female. Many of the life drawings were done on trips to Paris, at Colorossi's. The trips began when Moore was a student, and continued until the war. Back in their first year at the college, Moore and Coxon decided it would be pleasant to cross the Channel and look at some *real* Cézannes. They asked their principal at Whitsuntide, 1922, for permission to take the trip. Sir William was delighted, and gave them introductions to Maillol and Bonnard.

They never used them. They had brought no razor with them, were

Life Drawing, 1928

Ideas for Sculpture, 1928

dressed in army grayback shirts and looked disgusting after a day or two. Once they got as far as Maillol's door, but Moore said, "Well, he's working, and he won't want to be bothered," and they did not knock. Partly they were shy because the favorable rate of currency exchange made the English unpopular in France. They could have a seven-course dinner for one shilling threepence—about thirty cents then—and the French couldn't afford to go with them. And partly they were shy because their French was bad. On a later visit Moore went to a gendarme for directions. His friends watched a long scene in which Moore kept nodding his head while the gendarme spoke and pointed and spoke again and pointed again. After a final vigorous nod and a handshake, Moore rejoined his group. "What did he say?" they asked. "I don't know," he answered.

Every spring thereafter Moore and Coxon went over to Paris with a group of artists and art students. They took no buses or subways but walked everywhere. They drew in the afternoons at Colorossi's; in many of Henry Moore's old life drawings, you can recognize the chair the model used sometimes, a little, backless, plain chair. Sometimes the model would only sit a minute or two. At other times she would hold a

position for a long time, while Moore would turn out a variety of drawings from different angles or approaches. On occasion Moore drew so rapidly that, from the sound of pages turning in the sketch book, his friends accused him of reading secretly. Coming back on the boat train they propped their drawings on opposite seats in their compartments, and judged how well they had done on their holidays; sometimes one of them might come back with three hundred drawings.

In a sense, Moore drew all the models as if they were ideas for sculpture. They remained flesh, but when he drew he was not trying to be accurate, but to create monumentality. Sometimes he gave a thin model thick, strong legs. This Life Drawing of 1928, a ten-minute sitting perhaps, has a strange disproportion between face and body, not so much in size as in the degree of pictorial reality. The face is largely realistic, and more detailed than the body which enlarges unrealistically into a dream of stone. Moore uses the disproportion of styles as he later used disproportion of scale. The portrait-like face and the arms, which are also realistic, set off and emphasize the rocky massiveness of the body.

A fifteen-day excursion ticket cost thirty-seven and six, about $9, and defined the limits of their stay. Food, drink and shelter for two weeks cost about five pounds, or $25. Mornings in galleries, afternoons at Colorossi's sometimes until eight o'clock, and then they would eat and "have a booze-up. All very intense was that then," says R. V. Pitchforth, Moore's old friend from Leeds and the Royal College. "Cheaper than Brighton it was."

The annual excursions to Paris opened Moore's eyes to contemporary art. On the first visit he saw the Pellerin Collection of Cézannes, and was especially moved by "the triangular bathing composition with the nudes in perspective, lying on the ground as if they'd been sliced out of mountain rock. For me this was like seeing Chartres Cathedral." He looked at real Rodins for the first time, too, but in the early years Rodin was not primitive enough to be interesting. On later journeys Moore and his friends met French artists and kept up with what was happening. They did their bit, by their travels, to bring England into the twentieth century.

The trips survived marriages, divorces and everyone's changing circumstances. In 1926 Moore was best man at Raymond Coxon's wedding, and Gin and Raymond Coxon went to Paris married as they had gone single. Coxon moved out of the studio he shared with Moore, and he and his bride took the studio next door. Two years later Moore's fortunes took a dramatic turn when he accepted his first commission and had his first show. At the urging of Jacob Epstein, the London Underground asked Moore to do a relief on their new building at St. James's. It was a flattering invitation; Eric Gill and Epstein himself were doing other carvings for the same building; but Moore hesitated before accepting, out of skepticism about architectural sculpture. It seemed to him that too often sculpture on a building was merely decorative, and unable to live its own life. The architect Charles Holden persuaded him, asking him to "solve a problem." But Moore's doubts turned out to be well founded. The building is a slack piece of work, and Moore's North Wind is inferior to his other carving of the same period; it is relief, which Moore did not really believe in, and the distortion of style and scale makes an image, in this particular sculpture, which is like the work of fifty other would-be modern sculptors. It lacks inventiveness and individuality.

His show at the Warren Gallery was a happier occasion. Moore found Dorothy Warren a "person with energy and verve, real flair."

One year later she occasioned one of the most celebrated police raids in history by hanging the paintings of D. H. Lawrence. Moore sold ninety pounds ($450) worth of sculpture and drawings. More than the money Moore cherished the identity of the buyers: Augustus John, Henry Lamb and Jacob Epstein were three of them. Predictably, the *Morning Post* called him immoral.

But 1928 was even more important for a third event. Women were always important in Moore's life. Sometimes one of them went to Paris with him on the annual holiday, and in London there was a fairly rapid succession of beautiful creatures, but marriage never seemed close. One girl objected to taking second place to sculpture; another spent his money too freely, silly tactics in dealing with a Yorkshireman. Moore made up his mind that it was a bad idea for an artist to get married. You couldn't be married to carving and to a woman at the same time. Then he met Irina Radetzky, and it occurred to him in a flash, he says, that Rembrandt was married and Bach had twenty children.

Irina was born a Russian, in Kiev in 1907. During the Revolution she was separated from her mother, and remained with her grandmother for a short time until her grandmother died. She was twelve years old, one of the army of homeless children in post-revolutionary Russia. The Soviets had no sympathy because her parents had been rich. The daughter of an old socialist took her in, and allowed her to help teach young children in the school she was running. Irina's mother, widowed, had married an English officer and was living in Paris. Through the Polish Embassy (the Radetzkys were partly Polish and claimed for this purpose that Irina was a Pole) Irina was discovered and brought out of Russia to live with her mother and stepfather. Later she lived with her English stepgrandparents in Buckinghamshire. At eighteen she went to the Royal College of Art, a particularly attractive student of painting. "It wasn't as easy then as it is now to get to know students from other departments," Moore says, "but I was absolutely determined to get to know her, and when the chance came, at the end-of-term dance just before Christmas, 1928, I took it, although she had come to the dance with someone else." In fact she was engaged to someone else, too. "Irina lived in the country and the telephone played a great part in our courtship. Anyway, we were married in July, 1929."

As they were starting off for their honeymoon (which they spent in Cuckoo Cottage, in Dedham—Constable country) Irina tried to lift

At the beach, 1930

Wedding day

On holiday

Henry's suitcase at the station. She couldn't get it off the ground. It contained a block of alabaster, a piece Moore picked out because it was small. He carved it during their honeymoon, and sold it for sixty-five pounds ($325), which helped to pay the rent. The same alabaster Reclining Figure of 1929, eighteen inches long, recently took fifty-five hundred guineas ($16,500) at Christie's.

Irina stopped painting when she married. (Moore says she was very good at it.) Her aesthetic judgment expresses itself firmly but simply, over a drawing or a flower, in "that's nice" or "that's not very nice." She still has a slight accent, romantic and furry. She is a graceful and elegant woman nearing sixty now (when men who knew her in the thirties speak of her beauty then, their eyes water), and dresses with an unstudied chic. Irina has always stood to one side of the light of publicity, a very private woman. Her shyness has helped to protect her husband from the results of gregariousness compounded with fame. The house would be full of guests every weekend if it were not for Irina, and there would be no lonesome creative Sunday mornings. He would be flying to Mexico City for openings if Irina liked flying or openings. In the small living room at night she provides privacy and continuity in Moore's jagged and amazing life. During the visitors' part of the day, sometimes she slips around her garden surreptitiously, to avoid meeting more people.

(Many people have a different idea of Henry Moore's wife, and think that she is a health faddist and extraordinary walker, who set out to hike from California to New York. But Barbara Moore is not Irina Moore. Barbara Moore is an English subject, born a Russian, and describes her husband as a sculptor—so it is not surprising that people have confused the two. Her husband, actually an amateur sculptor, is a man named Harry Moore, which doesn't help at all. Once Barbara Moore called at Hoglands to apologize for the confusion.)

The end of the decade saw him married, and was the beginning of an intensely creative period. It began with the Leeds Reclining Figure of 1929, often compared with the Chac Mool that Moore saw on his return from Italy. But no one would ever mistake Moore's Hornton stone figure for a primitive work. The Mayan piece, except for the turn of the head at a right angle, all goes in one direction. It stretches out with two knees raised equally and the two arms similarly placed. Moore's Reclining Figure goes in contrary directions, its impulses neither linear nor circular, but resolved by opposition. The lady's left arm is raised, palm to the back of her head, so that her forearm is parallel to the lines of the bottom of the sculpture, but the upper arm juts away from the vertical. The right leg lies on the low parallel, but the left one rises and looms as high as the head and much more massive, dominating the sculpture. This looming of a part of the body became a signature, and appears as recently as the Lincoln Center piece of 1965.

The Leeds Reclining Figure was a personal breakthrough for Moore. He was aware all the time he was working on it—in his studio at the Royal College—that it was a major departure. For two or three years he had been impatient with the work he had done because it lacked formal variety. He felt that even Brancusi, whom he admired greatly, failed in not going beyond the single form. The human body could be separated into many units (head, forearms, feet—fourteen or more forms, depending on how minute you made the detail) and you could make these units interact. His earlier work, he felt, tended to be stiff and remote because it insisted on remaining a single form. Now he realized "that unless you had some tussle, some collaboration and yet battle with your materials . . . you are only behaving like the waves." A 1924 stone carving called Maternity had no neck, and the arms were buried in the body; Moore had restricted the forms in the pursuit of unity, and also for the sake of truth to material, to make the woman look more like a stone. But stones are not all boulders; later he was to tell of finding pebbles with "holes right through them." In the Leeds Reclining Figure, the left forearm gives us an anticipatory Henry Moore hole. The looming leg moves outward from the stone matrix. The breakthrough allowed Moore to move the human body out from Brancusi's egg, and yet through the massiveness of parts to remain true to stone.

Stone was his special love. In the Geological Museum he had seen a sample of Hornton stone among display cases of thousands of English minerals, and he liked the look of it. (Along with his scholarly knowledge of ancient sculpture, Moore is something of a geologist—at least among sculptors—and a botanist. He has carved in marble, painted slate, Hopton-wood stone, Portland stone, anhydrite stone, Bath stone, alabaster and Cumberland alabaster, Mansfield stone, Darley Dale stone, Ham Hill stone, ironstone, Ancaster stone, African wonderstone, verde di Prato, bird's-eye marble, travertine marble, Armenian marble, Corsehill stone, Pynkado wood, elm, ebony, beachwood, serpentine, walnut wood, boxwood and lignum vitae.) He took the name of the quarry from which the piece of Hornton stone had come, and wrote for a truckload of random blocks for his students. One of the random blocks became this Reclining Figure. Two friends helped Moore carry it into his studio. He was amazed by its hugeness in 1928; today it seems minuscule, only thirty-three inches long. It did not sell for many years, and was in his studio the night it was bombed in 1940. Moore finally sold it to the Leeds Art Gallery in 1941 for two hundred guineas. ("It represented exactly one-third of my income for 1941.") In the meantime Jacques Lipchitz had seen it at an exhibition in Zurich, and for the first time the Continent took notice of Moore.

The Moores returned from their honeymoon to take up residence in Hampstead, 11A Parkhill Road. A few yards away was a series of Mall Studios, where later Ben Nicholson and his wife Barbara Hepworth lived, and a number of other painters and critics. Geoffrey Grigson recalls "the Moores a bit hugger-mugger on one side of the road in the dust of their own manufacture, the Nicholsons along an alley in the lower side, in a studio of white space inhabited by circles and squares and fishing floats." Moore's studio was small and on the ground floor; a curved iron stairway from the sidewalk made it difficult to bring a big piece of stone or wood inside. He and Irina climbed further stairs to their tiny flat on the second floor. Since they had no money for objects, the flat was mostly bare; their only decorations were pieces of primitive art—old English pots, African and Mexican pieces—which they found mostly at the Caledonian market, the London flea market that was bombed out in the Second World War.

Moore set himself a target of thirty sculptures a year, mostly small; his Hampstead rent was more than half his income from teaching, and he needed to sell as many pieces as he could. If Irina in their sitting room upstairs heard the tapping stop in the studio below her, she called downstairs in her gentle accent, "Henery, you have stopped working?" At first—if he lacked impulse or imagination to work at the moment—he appeased her by saying that he was *thinking*. Later he learned to sit reading a book with one hand while he idly struck a block of stone with a mallet in his other hand.

They lived in comparative poverty for some time, relieved by high

Moore carving, 1927

spirits and good luck. The first car they bought had a leaky roof and irresponsible brakes. At the end of an early outing they returned to London in the rain, Irina sitting in the front seat with umbrella raised. They passed a policeman whose arm was raised to stop them, but could not stop because the brakes suddenly failed. Moore, not to be impolite, leaned out the window and called "Sorry!" as he passed the constable. The car stopped on a grade not many yards away. The constable strolled up saying *he*'d have been sorry if he hadn't been able to jump out of the way. He was writing out the ticket and asked Moore his profession. When Moore answered him he said, "Oh? Are you a sculptor?" and closed his ticket book and walked away. Moore accepted the favor as another bit of luck.

Perhaps half-a-dozen English collectors supported this corner of Hampstead. When one of the artists sold a painting or a carving, there would be a party in celebration. They played darts and shove ha'penny and ping-pong—Ben Nicholson invented a faster variant of ping-pong which allowed volleying—and drank what they could afford. They also played a game called "Shut-Eye Golf," at which understandably Nicholson and Moore excelled. They tacked a roll of plain paper to a table, and everyone drew shapes on it like islands or like a Paisley pattern, not letting the shapes overlap. It had to be possible to draw a line from one end of the paper to the other without touching any of the islands; but the player had to do it with his eyes closed. Moore would study the paper when it had been prepared, close his eyes and swiftly draw an immaculate line that avoided all obstacles.

Discussions and arguments were continual in the artistic Hampstead of the thirties. Writers lived there, or visited, too—Geoffrey Grigson, Adrian Stokes, Norman Cameron, Stephen Spender, and later Dylan Thomas. (When a London magazine asked Spender to sit for a portrait to their house artist, he said he wouldn't have his picture done unless the magazine could persuade Moore to do it. To his surprise, Moore agreed, and made three portraits in ink and chalk, good likenesses with intense eyes; they are the only portraits Moore has done.)

Artists and writers make good friends; writers like to visit the artist's studio, and envy the artist's physical work—the tapping of chisels, and the gooey mixing of paint. The poor writer must stand up from his desk and run around the block or build a model airplane to tire his body and busy his hands, before he creeps back to his narrow, intense blank paper. Sometimes the relationship can benefit the art of both parties, but in the thirties in Hampstead, the fine artists were far more avant-garde, closer to international modernism, than the poets and musicians. In France poetry and painting had been neck and neck since Apollinaire at least, but in England where painting had languished and poetry flourished for centuries, poetry was suddenly derrière-garde while the fine arts surged forward.

Hampstead was stimulating but it was time-consuming too, with its talk and its parties. Moore's solution was a cottage in Kent, where he spent all vacations from school-teaching. In 1931 Irina came into a small inheritance, and they bought Jasmine Cottage in Barfreston for eighty pounds ($400). It was a tiny Georgian building, particularly ugly, with two rooms downstairs and two up. The Moores knocked out the wall downstairs, leaving fireplace and chimney in the middle of the room. In the long summer holiday he liked to carve outside in the garden, where medieval stone heads from the porch of Barfreston Church looked over him as he worked. He made the concrete reclining figure there which is now in the museum at St. Louis, and had a terrible time getting it out through the gate.

Kent or Hempstead, he exploited his stone-carving breakthrough in a series of female figures: upright busts, reclining figures and mother-and-child figures. The mother and child is an old theme. The early ones are

Moore's drawing
of Stephen Spender

Maternity, 1924

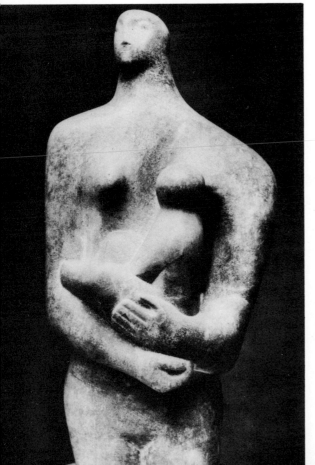

Mother and Child, 1931

lumpy; the 1922 Portland stone Mother and Child is almost square, the
child's head and the mother's head each broadly attached to the stone
matrix; the 1925 Hornton stone figure has the fat baby perched on the
head of his fat mother; his head forms the last and smallest of three
blocks: mother's body, mother's head and child's body, and child's
head. The Cumberland alabaster Mother and Child of 1931 is a
departure, and follows the 1929 innovation, detaching and contrasting
parts of the body. In this sculpture, just a foot and a half tall, the
contrast is most pronounced between the mother's tiny head and broad
shoulders, an early case of disproportion for monumentality. But the
contrasts do not end there. One shoulder is longer and lower than the
other, and this slant is paralleled by the slant of the arms and the
articulated fingers, holding the baby and spreading across the chest.
The slant moves upward as the whole figure does, from the tiny waist
widening out to big shoulders. Her small head has the effect of
stopping, or relieving, this motion. In another sculpture which he was
carving at Parkhill Road at the same time, the motion was downward
from a small head; he seems to have set himself a series of problems to
solve.

For Moore, the contrast of the mother's head and shoulders confers
monumentality, not predictably by formula, but subtly by minute
necessities encountered in the act of carving: This was the excitement
of working on this particular mother and child. (Later Jacob Epstein
bought it, which was another excitement.) He also enjoyed the material, Cumberland alabaster, which his sculptor friend John Skeaping
found on a farm in Cumberland; they knew no geological or local
name for the stone, and so named it for the county. The farmer turned
up odd chunks of it every time he plowed his fields, random shapes
which he sent down to London for carving. Moore prefers Cumberland
alabaster to ordinary alabaster (a material Sir Kenneth Clark compares
to processed cheese) because it has more color to it, so that the forms
are more easily seen.

This 1931 piece is not so much a breakthrough as a development,
one of a series of experiments suggested by the 1929 liberation of the
parts of the body. It is an early example of Moore's use of a small head,
a feature of his sculpture which had puzzled or irritated many ob-
servers. Some critics have wanted to call the diminished head anti-
intellectual, which Moore is quick to resent. "The head is the most

important part of a piece of sculpture. It gives to the rest a scale, a certain human poise and meaning; and it is because I think that the head is so important that I reduce it in size to make the rest more monumental." He resorts to his favorite authority. "Michelangelo's [heads] will sometimes go . . . twelve times into the length of the body," whereas the average head one meets goes about six and a half times into its average body. With the small head, as with truncated limbs on occasion, Moore is distorting the human shape for ends which are mostly formal, but which rely on the literary idea that a head is "so important." At the beginning of his release of the body from stone, the smallness of the head serves to emphasize the release. From the 1924 Maternity, whose head has no neck, he moves in 1931 to a mother whose head is all neck.

Also in 1931 Moore had a show at the Leicester Galleries, the first of many. The catalogue was generously introduced by Jacob Epstein: "Before these works I ponder in silence. The imagination stretches itself . . . Henry Moore by his integrity to the simple idea of sculpture calls all sculptors to his side. . . . For the future of sculpture in England Henry Moore is vitally important." (Many years later, when Moore's reputation finally outshone Epstein's, the older man became noticeably less gracious. When a collector in the fifties mentioned to Epstein that he was buying a Moore, Epstein reportedly asked, "Who's that?") The depression had taken its toll of collectors in 1931, and Moore's show (of three years' work) did well to gross 385 pounds (about $1900). The biggest sale was a Burgundy stone mother and child for seventy-five guineas ($392.50). An ironstone head sold for as little as eight guineas ($42).

Before each of the Leicester Galleries shows there was a private view day, which was another occasion for a party. In the days after the opening, while the papers were calling him names, Moore sometimes paced around Leicester Square all by himself, keeping an eye on the door of the gallery in the hope that someone would go in and buy something. His handicaps were not only the Depression and his own comparative youth but the intense Philistinism of the English public. (Though there is now in London a developing taste for modern art, the rest of England is unconverted; the educated middle class still tends to consider modern art a fad and a hoax.) That pejorative word "academic" has some meaning in England. By this time, no self-

Summer holiday: Ivon Hitchens, Irina Moore, Henry Moore, Barbara Hepworth, Ben Nicholson and unidentified friend

respecting modern artist is likely to join the Royal Academy if asked. One well-known artist was asked to join not many years ago; when he mentioned it to his dealer he was told that if he added R.A. to his name he could find another gallery. Successive presidents of the Royal Academy have blasted modern art from their pedestal. Sir Alfred Munnings, who made a fortune painting horses and huntsmen, was president of the Royal Academy from 1944 to 1949. Once he refused to set foot in an R.A. Summer Exhibition which showed a few tentatively modern works.

If the Leicester Galleries had wanted to paste up quotes from notices of Moore's first show, they could have advertised:

> Bolshevism in modern art.—President, National Society of Art Masters.
>
> Many, I fear, will come to laugh; few, I fear, will remain to pray.—*Evening Standard.*
>
> Wrong-headed.—*Apollo.*
>
> The cult of ugliness triumphs . . . it is almost impossible to believe that ["Reclining Figure"] came from the hands of a man of normal mentality.—*Morning Post.*

Opposition ran throughout the Establishment. A year later the *Times* reported that the Dean of St. Paul's was rewarded with laughter when he said at a dinner that these "modernist atrocities" would be "banished to the bathroom or even farther" within the next ten years. When J. B. Manson, Director of the Tate Gallery, asked Robert Sainsbury in 1938 for the loan of a Degas bronze, Sainsbury agreed on the condition that the Tate borrow and exhibit a Moore as well. Manson refused: Moore would enter the Tate over his dead body. And it was not only the obvious conservatives; the *New Statesman,* that bastion of advanced ideas, was more Philistine than the *Times.* As late as 1940, when Moore showed his great works of the late thirties at the Leicester Galleries, the *New Statesman* called them "exquisite chimney-piece ornaments . . . as deadly dry as late Stravinsky."

Moore has never responded to vilification; if hooligans tar and feather a bronze today, he thinks it's best to pretend he hasn't heard about it. But in the thirties the attacks had consequences. Even Sir John Rothenstein, when he was Director of the City Art Galleries in Sheffield early in the decade, was timid about showing Moore, whom he admired greatly. "The people there had never seen anything except 1850–1880 art. Therefore I borrowed things by Picasso, Rouault, and Italian primitives—but not by Henry Moore. I wanted to avoid controversy." (The Picasso was Blue Period.) Ultimately these attacks cost Moore his job at the Royal College. A note in the official chronology of his life, in the first volume of the *catalogue raisonné* of his work, says primly, "On expiration of appointment at Royal College of Art moved to the Chelsea School of Art." But the move was involuntary. It was in 1932, the year after his first Leicester Galleries show, that his seven-year appointment was up, that he moved over to Chelsea, where Raymond Coxon was already teaching, and where Coxon helped to establish him.

The *Morning Post* review of the Leicester show said that it was a scandal that the perpetrator of these monstrosities was allowed to pervert the young by teaching at the Royal College of Art. Moore's immediate boss, who was academic, took the article to Sir William Rothenstein and demanded that Moore be fired. Then the R.C.A. Old Students' Association, most of whom were art teachers, passed a resolution asking for the same thing. Moore had not minded the newspaper abuse (to be attacked by the nits can be construed as a

Moore in his studio, 1928

good sign) but now felt that he was a burden to his old patron Sir William. He offered to find a job teaching somewhere else (Chelsea had already approached him), and a little to his surprise Sir William accepted his offer.

In his first years as a teacher Moore was not always successful in preventing imitation. Outside the sculpture school of the R.C.A. in the late twenties, an old friend remembers, there were piles of rock-like mothers holding rock-like children over their heads. "They were exactly like Henry except they were terrible." The more he taught, the more successful he became at discouraging imitation. Some years after he had gone to Chelsea, a student applied for admission to the Royal College saying that he wanted to be a sculptor like Henry Moore. They asked him why he didn't go to Chelsea and learn from Moore himself. Oh, no, said the student; he had tried that and it was no good; Moore was too conventional a teacher.

The year 1932 was notable not only for Moore's resignation from the Royal College. It was the year of the Hole. As Henry Ford is famous for motor cars and Judas Iscariot for treachery, Henry Moore stands for the Hole. At one time there was a cartoonist's statues-with-holes-in-them category, like the psychoanalyst's-couch category, and the two-prisoners-in-striped-suits-talking-on-a-cot category. Moore is still identified among the unsophisticated as "the one with the holes." Yet he didn't invent the Hole. Michelangelo and Rodin and all good sculptors had made use of natural spaces, like the space between arm and head in Moore's Reclining Figure. The modern unnatural Hole—drilled right through a body—was the invention of Alexander Archipenko in 1912. But his Hole is small and decorative, a frivolous Hole. Jacques Lipchitz borrowed it and developed it later. Moore himself had carved holes before; he remembers keenly the excitement and the sense of discovery of the first cut through the block of stone. But the Hole did not *arrive* until 1932 in Hampstead, when Henry Moore finally exploited its potentialities and made it central to his work.

In an essay five years later, Moore defended the Hole by making three points about it. The first was negative, denying that holes were untrue to the material of stone: "A piece of stone can have a hole through it and not be weakened—if the hole is of a studied size, shape and direction. On the principle of the arch it can remain just as strong." (Since everyone has seen holes in trees he did not need to defend holes in wooden sculpture.)

The second argument was formal. To emphasize the three-dimensionality of stone you can do one of two opposite things: You can emphasize its weight by broad masses, embedding arms and head into body like early Moores, or you can open it up (natural or unnatural spaces) to give the sculpture depth. "By making holes through a block you can relate the front to the back." The second method is paradoxical —emptiness creates a sense of mass or volume—but it works.

The third argument, that of the "mystery of the hole—the mysterious fascination of caves in hillsides and cliffs," is only a hint, but it leads to a number of things. It is the first suggestion in Moore's writing that his figures may be metaphors combining woman and landscape. It is the first time that Moore has talked about the spiritual content of his sculpture; mystery is an element to be added to energy.

But mostly the Hole is simply a further opening-up of the block. It is the final ingredient in his bag of formal tricks and begins his total achievement of three-dimensionality. Too often his early work had been interesting only from one side and had lacked completion in the round. He felt as he grew older that his enemy was not the *Morning Post* or the Royal Academy or the Professor of Sculpture, but a long tradition of sculpture-as-relief, surface scratches as opposed to the creation of depth and mass. In any age, some arts will dominate others, and for centuries painting had dominated sculpture, driving it from the round into the flat. The 1929 Reclining Figure showed the way, and now the Hole was another step toward "that absolute, three-dimensional existence which is the object of sculpture."

5

1933–1939:
The Detroit
Reclining Figure

FROM 1933 to 1939 Moore did most of his carving in Kent. In 1934 they sold Jasmine Cottage and moved a few miles away to a cottage called Burcroft in the village of Kingston. Burcroft was nearly as small as Jasmine, but good land came with it. "I had five acres of shelving ground that ran down into a valley with hills on the other side. Any bit of stone stuck down in that field looked marvelous, like a bit of Stonehenge."

To a degree, Moore sketched or thought up ideas in London which he then executed in Kent. All the busy social life of Hampstead kept Moore on his toes. French artists kept paying calls—Braque, Léger, Hélion and at the time of the surrealist exhibition all of the movement's leading practitioners. Gradually the best of artistic England gathered there: Ivon Hitchens, Ben Nicholson, Barbara Hepworth, Adrian Stokes and in 1933 Herbert Read. Moore had met Read at the end of the twenties, when Read worked at the Victoria and Albert Museum; he visited Moore's studio and looked at the work assembled there, but went away without saying anything about it, which was his way. Moore was certain that Read had disliked it, and was surprised a little later to find in *The Listener* a Read article which praised him. In 1933 Read left his job at the University of Edinburgh and borrowed Moore's studio while Henry and Irina went to Italy. He lived among early Moores until he found a studio to rent nearby. A year later he published a book about Moore, nine pages of text and thirty-six plates. As chief resident critic, who picked up ideas from various ateliers, he was an invaluable promulgator of reputations in Hampstead.

Hampstead was "A Nest of Gentle Artists"—as Read called it, after Turgenev—but it was not an idea. If it was a party, it was more birthday than Communist. Its very importance, for insular England, was that it contained such opposites as Moore and Nicholson. Probably they did not feel themselves so opposed at the start. And from the start they belonged to the same groups. First there was the Seven and Five, an originally academic association which Nicholson (who liked organizations) joined and transformed. Then it was Unit One, a new group which published a collection of essays in a book called *Unit One*. The tone of the book is embattled and tough and confident. These differing artists—Moore, Ben Nicholson, Barbara Hepworth, Paul Nash—came together in fighting for "structural purpose" against sentimental "Eng-lishness" with its water colors of Cornish fishing villages. The book has little coherence to its aesthetic, but its tone is so spirited that one feels nostalgic for the antagonisms of thirty years back, when the Establishment had not yet decided to admire modern art.

Moore's essay "The Sculptor's Aims" set forth his ideas with headings and explanations:

Full three-dimensional realization. Complete sculptural expression is form in its full spatial reality. . . . *Vitality and power of expression.* . . . Between beauty of expression and power of expression there is a difference of function. The first aims at pleasing the senses, the second has a spiritual vitality which for me is more moving and goes deeper than the senses.

The essay ends with an apology for the mainstream of modern art:

Because a work of art does not aim at reproducing natural appearances it is not, therefore, an escape from life . . . not a sedative or drug, not just the exercise of good taste, the provision of pleasant shapes and colors in a pleasing combination, not a decoration to life but an expression of the significance of life, a stimulation to greater effort in living.

Unit One was a federation created under the fire of opposing forces. (To the president of the Royal Academy, Moore and Nicholson and their friends all looked the same, like Chinese to Westerners in bygone days.) The split within the unit was made obvious by the extremes of constructivism and surrealism. Constructivism arrived in England in the person of Naum Gabo, who had started the movement in Russia with his brother Antoine Pevsner and with Vladimir Tatlin. It was the sculptural equivalent of the contemporary suprematism of Kazimir Malevich, who painted the White on White which hangs in the Museum of Modern Art. (Both movements resemble Piet Mondrian, Ben Nicholson's greatest mentor, and Mondrian's De Stijl.) Constructivism is neither carved nor modeled but built up like a building: The nearest analogy is architecture. The 1920 *Constructivist Manifesto,* which Gabo and Pevsner wrote, renounces (as Mondrian renounced the curve) "volume as a pictorial and plastic form of space. We renounce . . . the mass as a sculptural element."

Nothing could be further from Moore's sense of sculpture, with its "full three-dimensional realization." Moore is organic while Gabo is mechanical; Gabo is geometric while Moore is natural. Constructivism has a content, too, which is far from Moore's concern with "power of

11-A Park Hill Road, Hampstead

expression" and mystery. "I do not experience any of the fear of the dark forces in nature which primitive man saw and experienced," says Gabo. "So long as our consciousness is with us, there is nothing destructive in them." Consciousness is the shield and the weapon, and "to be alive is to be awake."

A great deal of modern thought answers that when we are awake there is much of us that stays sleeping. Psychoanalysis, and the surrealism that grew out of it, grants to the dream a reality which only primitives used to believe in. Moore's creatures, independent of the formulations of surrealism, are expressions of a sleeping self. Part of his growth as a sculptor has been his progressive release from artistic models into an inwardness which expresses unconscious drives and desires. Moore has wished to exploit—to mine, to explore—the mystery within himself. Anything less than this expression, one feels, he would find ultimately superficial or decorative. Moore regards consciousness, on the other hand, as potentially destructive. He depends upon a theory of "universal shapes to which everybody is subconsciously conditioned and to which they can respond if their conscious control does not shut them off."

In 1935 Naum Gabo arrived in Hampstead, and in 1937 the Hampstead group published a book called *Circle*. A successor to *Unit One*, *Circle* is more nearly unified by a combination of constructivism and architecture. Gabo, Nicholson, Hepworth and Mondrian are joined by the architects Le Corbusier, Breuer, Neutra and Giedion. Henry Moore looks out of place, and feels out of place too; in his essay he sets forth less accommodating ideas about architecture than his fellow artists do:

Sculpture, more naturally than architecture, can use organic rhythms. Aesthetically, architecture is the abstract relationship of masses. If sculpture is limited to this, then in the field of scale and size, architecture has the advantage; but sculpture, not being tied to a functional and utilitarian purpose, can attempt much more freely the exploration of the world of pure form.

If he is stating the obvious, perhaps he needed to state it in order to convince himself. Though he was unconverted to constructivist theory, his most nearly constructivist work—stringed figures especially—dates from this period. Surrounded by abstract artists, he reportedly worried about the tendency of his sculpture to assume human form.

Shortly after he worked on his constructivist stringed figures, Moore showed in the huge International Exhibition of Surrealism in London. To say this of some artists would be to accuse them of stylistic opportunism, but Moore's constructivism was surreal and his surrealism constructivist. The surrealist exhibition "knocked everyone off the rails" in London, says one artist, but it didn't upset Moore. He had admired de Chirico and Giacometti for a long time, and was not surprised by what he saw. He had remained open to argument, which made him less liable to spectacular conversion from one theory to another.

But the exhibition forced everyone to take sides, though Moore lamented the necessity. A contributor to *Circle* wrote that the surrealist movement "depends essentially on introducing literary or formal content into formal composition," which was a vulgarism of course. Moore pleaded, "The violent quarrel between the abstractionists and the surrealists seems to me quite unnecessary. All good art has contained both abstract and surrealist elements . . . order and surprise, intellect and imagination, conscious and unconscious. Both sides of the artist's personality must play their part." One sees Moore as the good neighbor rushing between the fighting husband and wife, and taking blows from both. Eventually he had to choose, and he followed his natural preference for imaginative content over geometric form. He joined the surrealist group together with Paul Nash and Herbert Read.

In 1933 his second show at the Leicester Galleries had grossed a spectacular 700 pounds ($3,500). The collectors E. C. Gregory, R. J. Sainsbury and Sir Michael Sadler (who had opened his house to Moore, as a student at the Leeds School of Art, fourteen years earlier) were this time among his purchasers. His third and fourth Leicester Galleries shows grossed less—1936 made 470 pounds; 1940 made 465—but they were smaller to start with. In March 1936 the Museum of Modern Art in New York showed Moore's 1934 Pynkado wood Two Forms, in an exhibition called "Cubism and Abstract Art." It was Moore's first public showing in the United States. (He had been known to critics here for some time; Alfred H. Barr, now Director of Collections, had met him in 1927.) The 1935 catalogue, which Barr wrote, distinguished Moore from Ben Nicholson, who was also in the show, and who "attacks the problem of composing rectangles which had interested Malevich and his followers twenty years before. Moore's sculpture, indebted somewhat to the art of Picasso and Arp, is, on the contrary, organic in form with a sensitive feeling for the texture and color of his varied materials."

Barr wanted the museum to buy Two Forms, but lacked funds. He asked Sir Michael Sadler if he would like to donate it to the museum. Sir Michael replied elegantly: "With deep pleasure I do as you ask. The work of the Museum of Modern Art is of capital importance, and I prize the opportunity of having a part in the furthering of it. For the acquisition of the wood carving Two Forms by Henry Moore I enclose a cheque for . . . pounds." The museum never reveals what it pays for its purchases, but is able to say that the check was for less than fifty pounds ($250). In 1939 the Museum of Modern Art enlarged its Moore collection by buying the thirteen-inch lead Reclining Figure of 1938, which it had borrowed for an exhibition called "Art in Our Time."

These lead sculptures were cast late in the decade on the land behind Burcroft in Kent. Moore and his assistant Bernard Meadows improvised a foundry, which was merely a fire in an open field since lead has a low melting point. Meadows was Moore's first long-term assistant (earlier, another man had helped out in Kent for two months). He spent all vacations at Burcroft from 1936 until the war and assisted Moore again for a short time afterwards. For Meadows,

Reclining Figure, 1938

Two Forms, 1934

the arrangement took care of board and room during holidays (Moore could not pay him) and provided him with an apprenticeship in the art of sculpture. Later the apprenticeship all but stopped him doing his own work; to avoid being Moore-ish he stopped carving, abandoned the human figure for animal shapes, and reached for a content unlike Moore's. He is now Professor of Sculpture at the Royal College of Art; the British Council showed his work at the Venice Biennale in 1964.

They would arrive in Kent the night school closed—Henry, Irina and Bernard Meadows. The beds would be wet with the damp of an English house that has gone without heat for months, but there would be no time to air them out. "We'd crawl into the wet beds that night, and roll out of them carving the next morning." Moore remembers their typical day: "We'd all get up at 5:30 and . . . we'd go on with whatever work we'd been doing the day before. Irina got our breakfast at 6:30, and by 7:00 we'd be at work out in the open. . . . About 11:30 we'd get into our little Standard coupé and go down to the sea and bathe and eat our sandwiches, be back by 1:30 or 2:00, go on working until tea at 5:00 and then on again until dark. It often made a fourteen-hour day, right through the summer, but it was like a holiday, compared to London."

Three times a week they went to a film, mostly Hollywood things because Irina disliked Continental films and Henry didn't care what he

saw. Irina kept chickens in the garden, and occasionally Moore and Meadows poached pheasants or partridges or rabbits. They were too poor to go to pubs. The two men talked sculpture, painting and politics, while Irina cooked for them and looked after them. There was gaiety in the cottage, singing and joking and horseplay. There was also an incredible display of creative energy. Meadows felt, he says, as if he were living at the center of a hurricane. Moore did many of his best ideas-for-sculpture drawings there; when he was excited he would stay up drawing half the night. But mostly he carved. In 1938 at Burcroft he carved the stone Recumbent Figure which is part of the permanent collection at the Tate. In 1939 he carved the great elmwood Reclining Figure which is at the Detroit Institute of Arts. The surrealist-constructivist heads—squarish and highly abstract, with slots and rectangular protuberances for features—were carved there, and it was there that Moore did his first helmet heads.

His stringed figures were another innovation of the late thirties, but he made the first of them in Hampstead. The idea was another prize which Moore wrested from a London museum. The Science Museum, in Kensington among the cluster of the Museum of Natural History and the Geological Museum and the Victoria and Albert, has models that illustrate mathematical propositions. Some are solid, and look like any number of modern sculptures—even more like Brancusi or Arp than like Moore. Others are combined solids and strings. Moore's simple example is this: If you take a cardboard circle and a cardboard square, and make eighty equidistant holes around the perimeter of each, and thread strings back and forth from circle to square, the shape which the strings make halfway between the two pieces of cardboard will be a shape halfway between a square and a circle. Some of the propositions involve twisting the string a little; others involve two sets of strings, coming from different angles. In Bird Basket he carved the base in lignum vitae, and had to hollow out the ends in order to string it. Since lignum vitae is about the hardest wood there is, it took him weeks to carve it, and it is one of his few early carvings that he still owns. A magazine quoted him about it: "The string seems to add new tenseness and vitality to the form by contrasting, in its tautness, with the rounded wooden form and swirling grain of the wood."

The stringed figures are another step in the utilization of space in sculpture, like the beautiful iron work that Julio Gonzalez was doing in

France at about the same time. The strings emphasize the space between them and the solid base of the sculpture simply by containing this space. Moore did not continue this set of experiments for long. After doing eight or ten, he lost interest; they seemed too much a matter of invention rather than of imagination, and too readily decorative. Gabo, he feels, has since made beautiful, poetic structures out of the spatial idea of stringed figures.

The helmet heads were part of a series of heads that must include the verde di Prato Mask of 1924 and the Locking Piece of 1964. Many of the stringed figures were heads, too, though some were abstracted reclining or upright figures. Other themes he explored in these years were the bust, the mother and child, and the standing woman. But the reclining figure, starting from the 1929 Reclining Figure, remained his most common subject. A casual count in the three official volumes of Moore's work, *Sculpture and Drawings*, reaches more than eighty sculptures of the reclining figure. If he had five lifetimes, Moore says, he could not exhaust its possibilities. Some are neo-Mayan, some surrealist, some constructivist and some neoclassical; they are all variations on the same theme.

In the middle of the decade he did his first multiple-part sculptures, mostly as components of a reclining figure, like Four-Piece Composition of 1934. Upright two-parts, like the ironstone Two Forms of 1934, anticipated the family groups of ten years later. Nothing that Moore was to do in the next three decades would be without some origin in the sculpture of the thirties. Nothing is ever forgotten. Moore is like an animal who returns every year to the same series of landscapes, sniffing and feeling his way among the familiar and the new, bound by his nature to retrace his steps, to re-explore, to return every spring and fall to the same hill, the same valley, the same stream.

It was also in the thirties that Moore did most of his writing about sculpture, in the essays for *Unit One* and *Circle*, and in a few reviews and articles for *The Listener*. Though he wrote, "It is a mistake for a sculptor or a painter to speak or write very often about his job," he was unusually good at it. He writes about three-dimensionality: the sculptor "gets the solid shape, as it were, inside his head—he thinks of it, whatever its size, as if he were holding it completely enclosed in the hollow of his hand." He writes about truth to material: "Wood has a stringy fibrous consistency and can be carved into thin forms without

A mathematical model
from the Science Museum

breaking. . . . Negro carving . . . is religious, and, in movement upward and vertical like the tree it was made from, but in its heavy bent
legs is rooted in the earth." He writes about the properties of natural
form: "Pebbles and rocks show nature's way of working stone. Smooth,
sea-worn pebbles show the wearing away, rubbed treatment of stone
and principles of asymmetry. Rocks show the hacked, hewn treatment
of stone, and have a jagged nervous blocked rhythm. Bones have a
marvellous structural strength and hard tenseness of form, subtle
transition of one shape into the next and great variety in section. . . ."

92

Moore always found writing painfully difficult, but perhaps in the theoretical thirties it helped his thinking to be required to torture his sculptural ideas into syntax. In more recent years, he has put his thoughts into interviews. He responds to questioning seriously, hesitating painfully over the right word, leaning on his sentence with an intensity that creates precision. Answering so many questions about his beliefs and activities, he begins to substitute "one" for "I" automatically: "One gets up in the morning about seven-thirty . . ."

Trips to Paris continued throughout the thirties, though they were

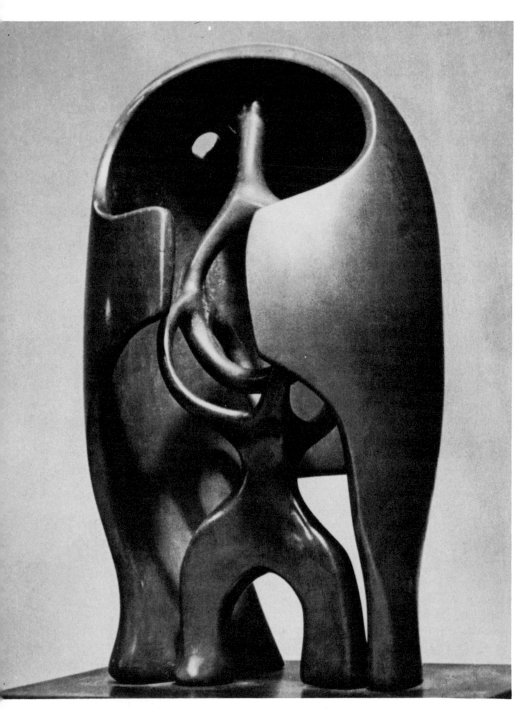

The Helmet, 1940

Sculpture, 1937

Recumbent Figure, 1938

more high-powered now. "When Irina and I were in Paris in the summer of 1937, Picasso invited a whole lot of us to go along to his studio and see how his 'Guernica' was getting on. There was a big lunch, with Giacometti, Max Ernst, Paul Éluard, André Breton, and Irina and me, and it was all tremendously lively and exciting and we all trooped off to the studio, and I think even Picasso was excited by our visit." The two men had met before and have met since; language impedes their relationship, but each has made his respect for the other known, Moore in part by emulation. "I remember him lightening the whole mood of the thing, as he loved to do. 'Guernica' was still a long way from being finished . . . you know the woman who comes running out of the little cabin on the right with one hand held in front of her? Well, Picasso told us there was something missing there, and he went and fetched a roll of paper and, with a twinkle in his eye, stuck a square of it in the woman's hand, as much as to say that she'd been caught in the bathroom when the bombs came."

Picasso needed to lighten "the whole mood" at his luncheon, because Guernica and the Spanish Civil War were subjects which he and his guests could not take lightly. The Hampstead artists were progressive and antifascist, and Hampstead was filling up with refugees from Hitler's Germany. In a book review as far back as 1935, Moore had denounced "the decadent art of the Babylonians and Assyrians, with their materialist and militarist society," in terms that sound as if he had been reading the *Daily Worker.* As the decade progressed toward war, Hampstead became increasingly political. Conversations which had been all aesthetic in 1932 were all political in 1937.

Moore considered taking time from his sculpture to devote to politics, but (like most progressives) found it difficult to act. He was member of a group that planned to go to Spain during Franco's revolution, a group that included W. H. Auden and Stephen Spender. The trip was for purposes of propaganda, though its ostensible purpose was to investigate Republican care of Spanish art works. They approached Parliament and were refused permission. Moore's politics, then and now, are inherited, untheoretical, English working-class Labor party. His name frequently appears on petitions against apartheid and for nuclear disarmament. He could no more vote Tory—though he is rich and has been surrounded by rich collectors for years—than he could model Toby jugs for tourists.

When war came in 1939 the continuity of his series of carvings was interrupted. But just at the start of the war he finished one of the greatest of his figures, the elmwood Reclining Figure dated 1939. The earliest sources of it in Moore's work are a series of ideas-for-sculpture drawings earlier in the thirties. The idea of a new opening-out of the Reclining Figure, using the Hole more audaciously than ever, had been growing in his imagination. The 1938 Tate stone figure was as opened-out as stone could be. Moore carved it originally for the garden of Serge Chermayeff in 1938; Chermayeff was buying it in installments, and when he decided to leave England for America sold it back to Moore, who sold it to the Contemporary Art Society, which later presented it to the Tate. The sinuous stone is rhythmic and fleshy, a natural object yet a mysterious one—in Sir Kenneth Clark's words both "the menhir and the memory of rocks worn through by the sea."

But Moore wanted more opening-out, and wood could go farther than stone. About the time he finished the Tate figure, in the summer of 1938, he found a good timber merchant in Canterbury, which is only a few miles from Burcroft, and bought a large elm trunk. He was ready to begin. As when he carved the 1929 Reclining Figure, he was conscious of making a breakthrough. And this time he was carving for a particular place. Berthold Lubetkin was the best young architect in England (he made the Penguin Pool at Regent's Park Zoo) and was building himself a penthouse which would have a long inset in one wall. Lubetkin asked Moore to "do him something" for the inset. (It was not precisely a commission, or Moore refused to look at it that way: He was doing it for himself; if Lubetkin liked it he could have it.) He was aware that a large Moore in Lubetkin's flat would be conspicuous, and it was the biggest piece he had ever attempted. He wanted it to be special, not "just the thing I was doing." By the time it was finished Lubetkin had suddenly given up architecture, had given up his penthouse, and had no place nor money for the sculpture. Moore had a large piece of elmwood on his hands.

The elmwood figure is nearly seven feet long. It undulates and gapes, feminine and tree-like, sensual and skeletal. By driving holes into the trunk, Moore makes the whole body into arm-like and leg-like units, solving the problem of the disunity of heavy trunk and spindly limbs. (He creates unity with the hole as well as discovering depth.) Also, there is a spatial resemblance between the natural holes—

beneath a raised knee for instance—and the artificial holes through the chest. The twin holes through the chest are breasts first of all. (Archipenko invented concave-for-convex some time before.) But they are also the space between arms and trunk; in this latter configuration the lady is wasp-waisted. All details are inventions, and all inventions are multiple. A short double wing of wood spans out to the sides of the figure from a sort of breast bone, and forms the front of the breast; a hole in the forward span is a nipple. But viewed from the thin side, this forward span is an animal head, the single hole standing for two eyes. Another invention is the hole in the middle of the head of the Reclining Figure; it is not deep, but as one looks at it from the front one has the sense of a long tunnel burrowing deeply. Moore has carved it so that it narrows gradually, revealing the chisel marks on the inside of the hole and creating the illusion of depth. When viewed from the other side, the hole gives the same illusion: Moore has narrowed each side toward the center.

This Reclining Figure moves us especially through a combination of apparent opposites: It is utterly sexual, a woman opening herself to a man; and it is at the same time a figure long decayed in the grave, an omen of our deaths. One psychoanalytical critic finds that "Moore's deepest theme is one of resurrection"; these figures are skeletons still partly clothed in shreds of flesh and tendon, and at the same time their wood or stone material is evidence of endurance and permanence: "One must look into the pit in order to look beyond." Frederick Wight starts from an expressionist premise: "Very strange forms are usually much more like what they represent than we first suspect." Moore's sculptures "take such forms as the psyche of the child wishes." Unconscious imagery expresses contrary things at the same time. There is the desire for permanence or resurrection; but also "the chest, or breast, is the feeding ground of the child, and it is only natural from the child's point of view that it should be eaten away. Of Moore's two 'obsessions,' the Mother and Child and the Reclining Figure, the latter is the more eroded, since the sculptor has not provided the woman with a child image, a part which he reserved for himself." The wish of the child's psyche is universal; Mother is the cake we all must eat and have.

The 1929 figure has perhaps more obvious force in its looming massiveness, but the Detroit Reclining Figure of 1939 is more subtle, more sensual, and more haunted. Behind it there is no Chac Mool or

Another view of the Detroit Reclining Figure, 1939

Arp or Lipchitz. In its grace and delicacy, one can see that it is nearer to classic form than the older sculpture—more like the reclining male Ilissus, a Parthenon pediment figure, in the British Museum—but it is no more Greek than it is Mayan. Discernible behind it is only a series of progressively opened-out Henry Moores.

When Lubetkin was unable to buy it, Sir Kenneth Clark (who visited Moore in Kent about this time, beginning their long friendship) cabled the Museum of Modern Art in New York that they could have a masterpiece for three hundred pounds, ($1,500). They did not buy it, and the Reclining Figure went unsold at the 1940 Leicester Galleries show. Moore took it back to his studio where it reclined among other unsold pieces, including its Hornton stone ancestor of 1929.

6

1940–1948:
The Madonna
and Child

THE Moores were at Burcroft in Kent when war started in 1939. Moore commuted to London to teach, but when the Chelsea School of Art was evacuated he resigned his position and stayed at the cottage. It was the end of his teaching. "When I stopped it, I knew I could never do it again. I hated term times, that breaking off of two days." Sculpture went on as usual in the autumn of 1939 and the winter of 1940. Moore finished the elm Reclining Figure alone, and cast several leads. Then in June came the fall of France. The phony war was over and an invasion of England seemed imminent. Casting about for a way to help, Moore returned to London and applied to Chelsea Polytechnic for training as a munitions toolmaker. "I was told sculptors could learn more quickly than the average person."

He waited in Hampstead for word that toolmaking classes were starting, but he heard nothing. Applicants were many and openings few. While he waited he was reluctant to begin a carving he might be unable to finish, so he concentrated on drawing. Eventually he knew he was not needed as a munitions toolmaker, but by that time he found it difficult to get proper pieces of stone or wood for carving, much less metal for casting. From 1940 to 1943 drawing was no longer "mainly . . . a help towards making sculpture," but an end in itself.

Possibly his enthusiasm for drawing was increased by a discovery he made just before the war. (It was a discovery for himself at least; it resembles techniques which other artists have used.) A niece of Moore's, Mary Howarth who was a daughter of his sister Betty, visited him in Kent, and asked him to make her a picture with her crayons and water colors. One of the crayons was white, and gave Moore the idea of putting in the main masses in white first. Sir John Rothenstein, in his book on English painters, explains the advantages:

Because the water-color recedes from the white wax, backgrounds can be put in almost instantaneously in broad, rapid strokes, and the white wax may then be worked over with pen and ink and water-color applied in small strokes; in case of failure the ink and water color applied to it may be readily washed off. . . . It is the use of white wax which enables him, by putting in the principle forms at the beginning, thereupon to model and refine them. The method, in fact, is directly analogous to his method as a carver.

103

The Moores were living in Hampstead when the Germans began to bomb London. They were still able to drive their car into town, when they left Hampstead in the evening, and so they were not aware that Londoners were sleeping in the subway stations for shelter from the bombs. (The Moores were unafraid and lucky.) "However, one night we'd been out to a restaurant and had gone by bus . . . and we came back by tube. That was the night that the first antiaircraft barrage was being put up in London as a defense against the night bombing. The air raid wardens at Hampstead tube station kept everyone inside until the all-clear." For the first time Moore saw "all the people settling down for the night, the thousands of shelterers who had been doing this for three or four weeks. . . . There were rows and rows of reclining figures," but his interest was more than formal: "Nothing like it had ever happened in the world before," he said later. "The only thing at all like those shelters that I could think of was the hold of a slaveship on its way from Africa to America, full of hundreds and hundreds of people who were having things done to them which they were quite powerless to resist."

He could not keep away, after that first night. "I used to go down different shelters, and make mental notes, just observing. Then the next day I'd draw them in my sketchbook." He filled a sketchbook and showed it to Sir Kenneth Clark, who arranged with the War Artists' Advisory Committee for Moore to do a series of large drawings from the sketchbooks. He spent most of 1941 making more than a hundred shelter drawings. Later he gave Sir Kenneth the first sketchbook; Irina owns a second one.

The exhibition of the shelter drawings in 1940 and 1941, followed by a Penguin Modern Painters called *Henry Moore* in 1944, which included six of them, began slowly to turn the tide of public appreciation in England. The drawings are representational, unlike ideas for sculpture, but they are not life drawings, and no one would ever find a likeness in them. He did not sketch on the spot, but sketched at home from memory; overnight his mind made the sleepers internal, strong expressions of our need for warmth and security in a dark tunnel. They are related to earlier Moores—mother-and-child figures, reclining figures—but they are more fragile and human than the carvings.

The color is intriguing. (Some sculptors use color like an architect's wash.) Geoffrey Grigson attributes some of its virtue to Moore's

Pink and Green Sleepers, 1941

Tube Shelter Perspective, 1941

observation of color in nature—the way lichen grows on rock, the color of worn stone—and adds, "Because he is so much free of having to say yes to objects, so he is more or less free of having to bargain with the color of objects. His objects, his lines, his ordering, freely represent his vision of life; by his colors he is freely represented as well." Titles of some of the compositions refer to this freedom, like Pink and Green Sleepers, where a light wash of green over most of the drawing is heightened by the red cloth on the arm of one of the two sleepers, far to the right in the picture. The drapery of the blanket is modeled, and the curves of the whole composition are strongly rhythmic; the curved hands carry out the curves of the drapery. Open mouths and nostrils gape (like caves or the Hole) and the sleepers are drowning in the curves that shelter them.

The drapery, and clothes, were new to Moore. Critics speak of his "Parthenon drapery," but he does not think that Greece was his primary source. "It was not until the blitz in London that I began to realize how deep-rooted the Italian influence had been. . . . My Italian trip and the Mediterranean tradition came once more to the surface." When Moore began sculpture again in 1943, he broke with his style of 1939, and used drapery and simplified human faces; the shelter drawings, with Masaccio behind them, entered his carving and modeling. The forties was his Italian decade.

Moore began the shelter sketches in Hampstead. When Ben Nicholson and Barbara Hepworth evacuated No. 7 Mall Studios and went to St. Ives in Cornwall, Henry and Irina Moore left 11A Parkhill Road to move into the Nicholsons' studio, which was considerably cheaper: fifty pounds a year instead of a hundred. In October, 1940 (Moore had been sketching shelters for a month), the Moores spent a weekend with friends in Much Hadham, Hertfordshire. When they drove back to Hampstead Monday morning they found their road blocked off because of an unexploded bomb. "I live here," said Moore. The policeman asked him the number, and told him that his studio was flat to the ground. It wasn't; he was mixing it up with another studio. But it was damaged, with doors off hinges, plaster down, tiles off and windows blown out. (Some sculpture was scratched but nothng destroyed.) It wasn't fit to stay in.

They called their friends in Much Hadham to tell them what had happened. It turned out that half a house was for rent in Perry Green,

the hamlet just outside Much Hadham. The Moores liked Hertfordshire and the country; London was unpleasant at the moment; and
Moore was no longer expecting daily to start his course as a munitions
toolmaker. They decided to take half of Hoglands for the time being,
keeping their places in Hampstead and Kent. They have not moved
since. (They rented out Burcroft during the war and sold it afterward.
They bought No. 7 Mall Studio later when they were prosperous, and
rented it to Bernard Meadows. Now they use it sometimes when they
go up to London.) At that time Hoglands was divided into two tiny
houses where farm laborers had lived for centuries, and it was decrepit.
The first night they slept there, fragments of antiaircraft shells rained
through the roof. Moore spent a lot of his early time at Hoglands
repairing the house. He made friends among the neighbors by instruct-
ing the Home Guard in the use of the bayonet.

They lived happily in the country—Moore making his shelter drawings—for some months, until the owner, who lived in the other half of
the cottage, decided to sell. Living by Moore's artistic earnings alone,
they were poor. They could afford to rent half of Hoglands but it
seemed impossible that they could buy the whole of it. The price was
nine hundred pounds, one-third down. Then, "One day I had a check
in the mail, a complete surprise, it was the biggest sale that I had
made." It was a check for three hundred pounds for the 1939
elmwood Reclining Figure, from Gordon Onslow-Ford. (Onslow-Ford
had seen the sculpture at the Leicester Galleries show, on sale at four
hundred pounds; when the show closed with the Reclining Figure
unsold, he thought he might be able to pick it up for three hundred.)
Like many artists Moore had developed a trust in his luck; this nick-of-
time check has always seemed to him to bear out his trust. "That is
how we are here," he says now, "in exchange for that piece of
sculpture." Onslow-Ford loaned it to the San Francisco Museum for
many years, and in 1965 sold it to a donor (who gave it to the Detroit
Institute of Arts) for about seventy-five times what he paid for it. But
no amount now could be as large to Moore as the three hundred
pounds when he needed it in 1941.

The shelter drawings were so successful that when they were finished Moore looked around for another subject connected with the
war. Herbert Read came up with an idea that sounded perfect: Moore
would visit coal mines and do a series of drawings that memorialized

this portion of the war effort. It sounded good for any number of reasons: Miners, in the heat of the mines, worked nearly naked, their bodies sufficiently monumental; mines were tunnels, like subways and like the Hole; miners cut into stone like a sculptor; and Moore would be connecting to his childhood through his father's occupation. The War Artists' Advisory Committee sent Moore to Castleford in January, 1942. (He had returned only once since coming to London, in 1938 when he had been guest of honor at a reunion of Secondary School alumni.) He stayed in a pub for two weeks, going down into the mines every day, and never saw Castleford at all. It was dark and foggy when he went down to the pit in the morning, and dark and foggy when he rose up at the end of the shift; the dimmed-out streetlights only lighted up a few yards of fog.

He had never been down a mine before. "It made clear many things about my own childhood . . . and made me learn more about miners —but I didn't find it as fruitful a subject as the shelters. The shelter drawings came right after first being moved by the experience of them, whereas the coal mine drawings were more like a commission. . . . [They] were two weeks' physical sweat seeing the subject, and that number of months' mental sweat trying to be satisfied carrying them out." The miners did not enter Moore's imagination and emerge transformed, the way the sleepers did. His drawings of coal miners hacking at the pit face are good pictures, with a muscular human energy to them, but they mean no more than what they represent. (If there had been women coal miners at the seam, Moore would have made them internal and eternal.)

He returned to sculpture in 1943—he was able to get stone by that time—though drawing continued to be an important part of his artistic life for another decade. He returned to sculpture by what seemed at the time a strange departure, executing a Madonna and Child for a church. Although Moore had begun to receive some official attention, it took an unconventional churchman to suggest that he do religious sculpture. Canon Hussey, then of the Church of St. Matthew's in Northampton, also commissioned, at different times, a cantata by Benjamin Britten and a painting by Graham Sutherland.

Moore was at first hesitant, and as usual would not accept the proposition *as* a commission:

At the Coal Face, 1942

I wasn't sure whether I could do it, or even whether I wanted to do it. One knows that Religion has been the inspiration of most of Europe's greatest painting and sculpture, and that the Church in the past has encouraged and enjoyed the greatest artists; but the great tradition of religious art . . . has fallen very low (as anyone can see from the affected and sentimental prettinesses sold for church decoration in church art shops). . . . I could only promise to make notebook drawings from which I would do small clay models, and only then should I be able to say whether I could produce something which would be satisfactory as sculpture and also satisfy my idea of the "Madonna and Child" theme as well. . . . I began . . . considering in what ways a "Madonna and Child" differs from a carving of just a "Mother and Child"—that is by considering how in my opinion religious art differs from secular art. . . . The "Madonna and Child" should have an austerity and a nobility and a certain touch of grandeur (even hieratic aloofness). . . . I have tried to give a sense of complete easiness and repose, as though the Madonna could stay in that position forever (as, being in stone, she will have to do).

Canon Hussey thought of asking Moore for a Madonna when he saw the exhibition of shelter drawings, and the finished sculpture bears out what he imagined. The folds of the Madonna's dress—the first drapery Moore ever carved—remind one of the shelter drawings, and so do the simple and generalized faces of the two figures. Of course it is a variant of the mother-and-child theme, and the simple but representative facial features have antecedents in some early work, but the Madonna and Child is a departure all the same. It is not a formal departure—there is little formal inventiveness of any kind—but a change in feeling from the earlier carving. Here for the first time the tenderness in Moore is more obvious than the toughness. As the rocky, primitive women of the twenties represented his extreme of harshness, the flesh of the Madonna represents his extreme of softness. Drawings showed the way, but perhaps the move from Hampstead contributed to the change. Now Moore lived in the country, away from urban rectangles among the soft hills of Hertfordshire; the constructivist city gave way to the organic countryside. More important perhaps, he no longer lived

Reclining Figure, 1945–1946

Reclining Figure, 1945–1946

among the theorists of the abstract, Gabo and the Nicholsons. When the theories left, the landscape was there instead.

But Moore himself sees the change as less clear-cut. He is used to people who *either* admire his Madonnas and family groups while they deplore his abstractions, *or* who admire his least representative carvings and despise his humanist figures. As he did when he confronted the quarrel between surrealists and constructivists, he likes to contend that both sides are necessary to sculpture, and that at times he has simply desired to let one side dominate the other. He says of his abstract work, "Even while I was doing it, I knew that I was isolating one aspect of sculpture, and that that part could not contain everything." His sculptures have tended to include disparate elements—figurative, geometric, surreal—which other sculptors isolate; and when his work begins to represent one idea chiefly, something in Moore pulls back, and goes in another direction. One extreme by itself is cold; the other by itself sentimental; together they make good sculpture. Sometimes he has held himself in balance by carving different personal extremes at once: In 1946 he carved the Dartington Hall Reclining Figure (which is representational and draped, and bears family resemblance to the Madonna) at the same time as he carved the elm Reclin-

111

ing Figure which is at Cranbrook Academy in Bloomfield Hills, Michigan—a surreal development of the 1939 elm Reclining Figure, with a vestigial inner piece like a child in the womb. The Dartington Hall woman reposes classically. The Cranbrook figure, in the words of a critic, struggles "out of the earth like a tree." The simple features of the former contrast with the simplification of the latter, where a single slot across an elmwood head accounts for all features at once.

These two figures helped to make 1946 another *annus mirabilis*. The greatest miracle occurred March 7, 1946, when his daughter was born and named Mary after his mother and sister. Mary's birth gave an impetus to the tender side of Moore, and there were drawings like Two Women Bathing a Baby, returns to the Mother-and-Child theme, and developments of the family group, a theme he had dealt with fleetingly before. Henry was 47, Irina 39; earlier there had been a series of miscarriages, and Irina was ill when Mary was born, but for both of them the event was enormously happy, and they have doted on their daughter. When she was little she played in bed with her parents every morning. She attended a local day school until she went away to boarding school at twelve. Moore once flew home from an opening in São Paulo because Mary was ill. As his father made plans for him, Henry Moore sets out a course for his daughter. Mary has been painting since she was a baby, and wants to go to art school. She has attended the Slade one day a week for one term, but not more than that. Her father wanted her to go to a university first, at least for a bit, because he says that when she goes to an art school she'll never learn anything else. So far the father's will prevails; Mary went up to St. Anne's College, Oxford, in October, 1965.

The Dartington Hall and the Cranbrook reclining figures were shown at the Leicester Galleries, together with other recent work, in October of 1946. Two months later the Cranbrook piece was among the most recent of Moore's sculptures shown at his Museum of Modern Art retrospective in New York. This exhibition initiated the postwar international boom in Henry Moore, and the museum must receive some of the credit for his reputation—as it must for the reputation of most contemporary artists. For one thing, the tribute of a New York retrospective helped to convince some members of the English public that they had an artist in their midst.

The museum had shown and bought Moore sculpture in the thirties, and during the war had the safekeeping of the Tate Recumbent Figure. When the war started the sculpture stood in the British pavilion at the 1939 New York World's Fair. Sir John Rothenstein arranged that it be lent to the Museum of Modern Art for the duration, and it was a popular piece for nearly six years in the sculpture garden. But then it almost caused an international incident. In 1944 vandals climbed into the garden over the Fifty-fourth Street wall. The Recumbent Figure was discovered in the morning pushed from its pedestal, its head broken off at the base of its neck. The damage was repaired, though one can still see the scar. News of the vandalism was suppressed under wartime controls in England, lest the destruction of this "modernist atrocity" be deemed anti-English.

The 1946 retrospective came five years after Moore's only earlier retrospective, a smaller exhibition staged by Philip Hendy at Temple Newsam outside Leeds. The New York exhibition showed fifty-eight pieces of sculpture and forty-eight drawings borrowed from galleries and private owners in England and America. James Johnson Sweeney wrote an extended essay on Moore for the catalogue. American critics were enthusiastic. The *New York Times* critic praised Moore's "complete integrity" and followed the daily review with a Sunday article. Later *Life* had four pages of pictures and a bit of text about Moore ("He now gets very good prices for his work, which sell for $1,000 to $8,000"), and a little essay by Noel F. Busch cajoling the public into tolerance of modern art. After New York the show traveled to Chicago and San Francisco; virtually the same show went on to Australia.

Moore flew to New York for the exhibtion, his first visit to the United States. He found it exhausting. The night before the show opened he met the New York art world at a party and his voice left him, a symptom which had occurred before; Moore attributes it partly to Cambrai gas, and partly to nervous terror. One thing he enjoyed, besides his success: He made friends with his American dealer, Curt Valentin, who had been responsible for much of his earlier reputation in the United States. Valentin was almost unique among dealers in working for modern sculpture, and represented Maillol, Arp, Marini, Lipchitz, Marcks and Calder, as well as Moore. He first heard of Moore from Lipchitz, and wrote him in 1942, asking for drawings to exhibit. The British Council sent them across the Atlantic by diplomatic courier.

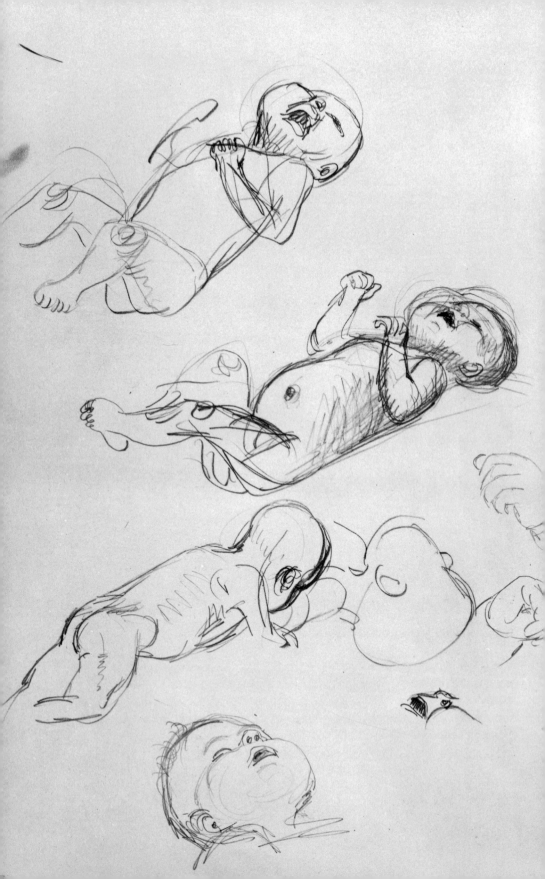

Family Group, 1946

As soon as Moore met him, "I began to count him as my friend as well as my dealer. . . . He looked after me as if I was a near relative. Every day at 8:30 A.M. he telephoned my hotel to know my program, my problems, and in what way he might help throughout the day." Valentin's attentions continued when Moore returned to the rationing

Studies of the Artist's Child, 1947

of postwar England. Moore wrote a letter in 1947: "This morning a food parcel arrived. . . . Irina was delighted with what it contained and she was very pleased that there was some soap for bathing Mary, our baby, with. Baby toilet soap, Irina says, is impossible to get in Bishop's Stortford or in London." About this time Valentin bought a Hillman Minx in New York and shipped it to Perry Green; it seems an odd way for an Englishman to buy a Hillman, but it was the only way. The cable read, "Your mink is on the way," by mistake, and Moore was frightened that his request had been misunderstood.

The British Council has also been highly effective in making Moore's international reputation. The organization exists to promote the literature, music and fine art of the United Kingdom all over the world, and is supported by government money. (The United States has no comparable institution.) The British Council, which began in 1934, but operated in a large way only after the war, organized the 1947 Australian tour of the Museum of Modern Art exhibition. When the exhibit reached Australia, the Council had three months' notice to prepare an exhibition for the 1948 Venice Biennale. Many countries showing at the

A section of the Museum of Modern Art Retrospective, 1946

The Moores in 1946

Biennale exhibit more than one artist in a category, and thus compete against themselves. The centralized British Council decided to send only its best old artist and its best new one. A Turner exhibition was touring the Continent at that moment, so they routed it south. The best possible Moore exhibition was out of reach, so they set out to gather the second best. Though they have made up many Moore shows in the years since (now they have a permanent collection of Moores, which they rotate from continent to continent), the first that they assembled was the most important.

In three months they put together a hodgepodge of new sculptures and old ones which had not made the trip to New York. Though the conglomeration was inferior to the carefully prepared exhibition of the Museum of Modern Art—it was weak in the "breakthrough," strong in "just the thing I was doing"—it won Henry Moore the International Sculpture Prize. A year and a half after the Museum of Modern Art retrospective, the prize at the Venice Biennale was canonization following immediately upon beatification.

7

1949–1957:
The King and Queen

AT Hoglands in Perry Green, the sculptor worked at his art, as one of his friends put it, "in such a sensible way, like a chicken farmer." Some of the neighbors had been after him for years to leave a mark on the village. When the West porch of the Much Hadham Church was being repaired, Moore carved conventional heads of a medieval King and Queen to replace some recent poor cement casts. He didn't carve Moores for fear of spoiling the integrity of the church. Most of the inhabitants of Perry Green are just waving acquaintances, some from the period when the far room was not a studio but the village shop. (Moore had five pounds a year rent for it until it closed early in the fifties, and didn't evict the shopkeepers because people depended on the shop.) Few of his local acquaintances have been artistically sophisticated. Most tend to say that they like "the man more than the work, don't you?" and pay him the dubious compliment of saying that he is "not like an artist at all."

There is a tranquillity to him, which is unlike the usual picture of the artist. He once smoked a hundred cigarettes a day (he gave them up in 1943) but he seldom seems unduly nervous. He does not enjoy being forged (one man, so far, has made and sold a few "Moore" drawings), but otherwise he seems remarkably unegotistical. If one of his neighbors goes out walking with him, the conversation may touch on almost anything in the world, but it doesn't touch on Henry Moore or on sculpture unless the neighbor brings it up. But sometimes, walking along and talking in a careless way, he will suddenly kneel down and pick up a stone with a peculiar shape.

He never stops looking for significant form. "I contend that every form, every shape, every little bit of natural object that you pick up, every chip off a sculpture has got a meaning, if you can find it." It was not only little things (it was also dinosaur bones and cliffs with caves in them), but little things are easier to take inside, perhaps to the far room itself, to ponder the meaning, "if you can find it." There has to be a readiness for the particular form. In the summer vacations when Mary was a little girl the Moores went to Broadstairs in Kent, and Henry and Mary used to look for crabs on the shore frequently, because she loved it and it gave him an excuse to look at pebbles. "Sometimes for several years running I have been to the same part of

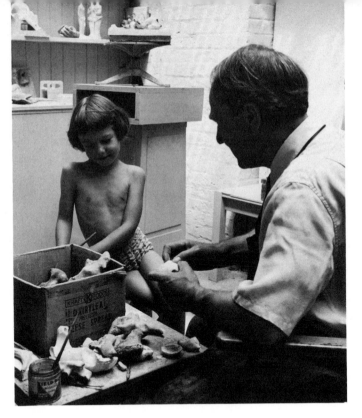

Mary and her father

the seashore—but each year a new shape of pebble has caught my eye, which the year before, though it was there in hundreds, I never saw. Out of the millions of pebbles passed in walking along the shore, I choose out to see with excitement only those which fit my existing form interest." By this time Moore's reputation as a pebble collector is world-wide, and he frequently receives boxes of shells or unusual rock formations by mail; they seldom fit his existing interest.

His form interests fluctuated and expanded, and returned to old themes with new shapes. In 1950 he did another series of heads, helmets with interior pieces (of which most were also abstractions of the mother and child) and openwork heads, delicately latticed faces that emphasized space. In 1950 he made his three rocking-chair figures, each of them a mother sitting in a rocking chair, which really rocks, holding a child aloft. The chairs are ladderback, frail strips of bronze horizontal across bronze uprights. The slats are so delicate that it would have been impossible to carve them in stone, and impractical in wood. Moore could not have modeled them in clay or plaster either, the way he normally models. To use such thin forms, Moore had to model directly in wax—a technique he discovered for himself in his

122

Rocking-Chair Figures

lead foundry in Kent before the war—and have a single cast made from the model. (Five further casts were made from each original rocking-chair figure.) Wax has a tensile strength which allows it to be stretched thin.

By 1935, he remembers, he had already found the limitation to stone or wood too restrictive, and was sketching ideas for metal sculpture. But he was modeling more and more now, after the war, and it was not only because of the formal liberation. His old dogma about the superiority of carving had worn out its usefulness; once it had been most useful, and pervasive among modernists. When Epstein (whose best work eventually was bronze) met Gaudier-Brzeska in 1910, Ezra Pound says, the "scowlings of Assyrian sculpture" entered Epstein's "tone and eyebrows," and he said, " 'UMMHH! Do . . . you cut . . . direct in stone?' 'Most certainly!' said Gaudier who had never yet done anything of the sort. 'That's right,' said Epstein, 'I will come around to your place on Sunday.' So Gaudier at once went out, got three small stone blocks, and by working more or less night and day, had some ready by Sunday." The same question was being asked at the end of the thirties, when Henry Moore met Wyndham Lewis for the first time.

Moore and a friend waited for him at a table, and suddenly Lewis strode up in a black hat asking, "How do you carve? Direct?"

Modern art in general, with its emphasis on the medium, has valued the ability of the artist to work in his material. That Brancusi began life as a cabinetmaker and Braque as a decorator has been a point in their favor. The idea of truth to the material of the medium is deduced from architecture: Treat stone as stone and steel as steel. The analogy to sculpture is simply made, and in carving one takes advantage of the natural grain, surface and texture of the wood or stone. The dogma was current on the Continent, but more in theory than in practice. In England the idea was anticipated by the arts and crafts movement, and underwritten by the medievalist ideas which passed from William Morris to Eric Gill; critics like Herbert Read and R. H. Wilenski championed carving with an intensity more theological than aesthetic.

There *is* a difference between taking away and building up. The carver must have an idea to cut down to, and in Moore's phrase must "collaborate with the stone" as he uses his chisel. But in most critical writing about carving there are the accents of moral superiority, and an artistic irrelevance of *hard work* is an unacknowledged part of the argument. Much of the case for carving is puritanical. Moore discounts it now. "The workmanship which people like Eric Gill thought so important can degenerate into a most awful mental laziness, like knitting or polishing the silver." He still thinks it good training for a young sculptor to carve, because in carving you can't get away with something that doesn't exist, and you must be deliberate because if a thing goes wrong you can't rub it out. But really he doesn't "think it matters how a thing is produced, whether it is built up, modeled, welded, carved, constructed or whatever. What counts really is the vision it expresses. . . ."

Forty or fifty years ago, perhaps the vision could not have been expressed except in carving, because of the *associations* of modeling. Though the attractions of wood grain and stone texture exist, the attack on modeling was mostly irrational. Such irrationalities are necessary from time to time. Modeling had come to mean academic, romantic and pseudo-Greek. Proponents of carving attributed to technique what was really formal and spiritual change, an opening-up of the imagination in mass and volume, three-dimensional form.

There are parallels in other arts. When a live new movement in poetry overthrows a dead orthodoxy (live Dryden and dead followers of Donne; live Wordsworth and dead followers of Dryden; live Eliot and dead Wordsworthians), it requires a new technique, not because the real material has altered, but because conventional dead associations have accrued to the old technique. Some vers librists contemporary with Epstein contended that vers libre was the only way to write a poem: They were trying to shake off the sonnet dust that covered them. The nakedness of vers libre, the necessity to improvise by ear, provided the necessary stimulus, and good art rode out of bad theory. Any new or rediscovered technique (free verse or lucite or syllabics or junk-assemblage or carving or Anglo-Saxon meters) can suggest new forms. Car fenders may provide new ways to represent a woman's body.

Yet it doesn't necessarily follow that the sculptor models, just because the battle for three-dimensional form has been won and it becomes *possible* to model. Many of Moore's recent bronzes could have been carved in stone, as far as technique goes. Moore's almost total switch to modeling has a complex of explanations. It's not the hard work of carving; he finds carving relaxing. It's not to make money; taxes help to make sure that he gets little more from five bronze copies than he would for a unique stone. But he can afford to model now, which he couldn't when he was young, and since he models he can keep one copy of everything, which is both a pleasure and a help to further sculpture. Also, making several copies of each sculpture helps to spread his work around the world: A big bronze can exist in England, Germany, the United States and Brazil at the same time.

But the most important source of the change is inside Moore, and arises from his sense of the conflict between creative energy and approaching death. "The difference between modeling and carving," he said in 1960, "is that the modeling is a quicker thing, and so it becomes a chance to get rid of one's ideas." Most of his friends date this eagerness from a mild illness in 1954. He had not been ill since he had been gassed in 1917, and his hospitalization at fifty-six seemed to remind him that he was not immortal. In the far room now there are three pieces of marble, originally planned as a three-part carving, now a two-part and a separate single piece. Three years ago Moore took the marble and a little maquette of his idea on holiday with him. He relaxed, not having to think, and chipped away until the forms almost reached the shape he wanted, but with a rough finish. Unsmoothed and unpolished, they have a faceted dusty surface like plaster. Now Moore wonders if he will ever finish them. He believes that to be true to the material he must finish the surface and show the quality of the marble. Yet to do so, he would have to spend two weeks, full time, and he does not want to take that long from the remainder of his life.

He is still a carver, even when he models. The gesture of his bronzes, with their "holes right through them," suggests carving. He uses plaster instead of clay because he can hack away at it like a carver, chopping with an ax sometimes. When a plaster is almost ready for casting, he likes to make final marks on it, and when he works over a wax, or patinates a bronze that has come back from the foundry, he is putting his carver's mark upon the bronze. One of his critics finds that his modeled surfaces suffer because of his carver's vision. "Stone automatically has an interesting surface—his stone had a *radiance*—and bronze does not. So Moore tries, artificially, to liven the surface of his bronzes with irrelevant markings." Most of his old friends are unanimous in their preference for the carving. "Too many inferior people are having a go at his things," said one old painter. "I saw some drapery on one of his pieces a little while ago and I don't know what it was, but it wasn't Moore's drapery. I wish he'd sack the lot of them out there, and live quiet and carve, and turn out one a year." But old friends are notoriously unable to admire the later works of the young genius they knew.

In 1952 Moore decided to learn more about the founder's technique by building his own foundry at the bottom of his garden. He never intended to cast many pieces there—it was not a device to save money—but wanted to understand the process, in the hope that it would give him some formal ideas. With two assistants and a neighbor he made a miniature foundry, a kiln about four feet square. He cast eight or ten pieces and that was enough. His neighbor remembers helping to raise the temperature of the coke fire all one day. The bronze would melt at 1940 degrees. They took turns slogging away at the second-hand pair of blacksmith's bellows, and at nightfall the bronze finally started to melt and they had to leave it because it was too late. Moore's bronzes are made mostly by the lost-wax process.

The founder first makes a negative cast of the original plaster, and from this casts a wax model which is to be identical with the final bronze. The wax is about three-eighths of an inch thick, stiff, about the texture of candle wax, and usually brick red. The founder removes any obvious seams and distortions of the surface of the wax, but then Henry Moore must put the finishing touches to it. Every maquette in an edition is unique, albeit minutely. With a big piece, Moore must visit the foundry to do the job.

When the sculptor has finished with the wax, the founder covers it, inside and out, with another negative cast of "grog"—a mixture of plaster and powdered stoneware which resists heat. The resultant lump is put in a kiln—some foundries build a new kiln each time because there is such a variety of shapes—and baked for about three days. The wax runs out through a hole in the bottom, and the grog bakes until it can contain the heat of molten bronze. While the negative cast is losing all its wax, the bronze ingots are melted. When you drop one in a bucket of molten bronze it swims and diminishes like an ice cube with hot tea poured over it, only it takes about thirty minutes to disappear. Two men lift up the bucket of hot metal with great pincers, one man on each handle, and set it down in a metal hoop which has long handles on each side. Then they carry the bucket like a chaired emperor to the negative cast, which is sitting upright with the hole on top, awaiting its impregnation. The negative cast must have air holes and runners and all manner of tricks if the bronze is to fill exactly every touch of the sculptor's fingers. But a good bronze founder can reproduce anything. Picasso's Bathers was knocked together out of cheap boards like the sides of packing cases, and the saw left a hairy surface of soft wood, but the bronze is perfectly faithful to these tiny tufts. After the bronze has hardened, the founder knocks off the grog with a hammer, and the sculpture is released.

The year of the foundry, which signified his conversion to modeling, was also the year of his biggest carving to date. Moore likes such indications of flexibility. He carved a screen for the top of the Time-Life building in London. "It seemed to me that the Screen should look as though it was part of the architecture, for it is a continuation of the surface of the building. . . . The fact that it is only a screen with space behind it, led me to carve it with a back as well as a front, and to

The Time-Life Screen in process

pierce it, which gives an interesting penetration of light, and also from Bond Street makes it obvious that it is a screen and not a solid part of the building."

The Screen is composed of four large stone panels set in a stone frame. Each panel is a separate abstraction, harking back in their style to the surrealist slotted head forms of the late thirties. Some ideas-for-sculpture drawings of the thirties clearly anticipate the Screen. His best idea was to make the panels movable—not in the wind like a mobile (they each weigh two tons) but shovable with a crowbar at least. Many pedestrians would walk past the building frequently, and this would give them something to keep on looking at, "if each of the four motifs could, on occasions, be turned, i.e., put at an angle to the surface of the building." He thought in terms of a new angle every two months.

He set about trying ideas for the panel, and modeled a series of motifs (some of the rejected ones have been cast as maquettes) until he found the right combination of four. He made a working model in plaster, forty inches long, which he later cast in bronze. (The Screen was the first of his ideas to be done in three sizes.) Then he and his assistants carved the stone, in the winter of 1951–1952, on scaffolding in the big front yard of Hoglands. (Moore had not yet bought the new land behind the house.) His neighbors—and postmen and delivery boys and taxi drivers—saw Henry Moore at work, as they had seen him when he carved the Three Standing Figures in 1947. While they watched the Screen take shape over the winter, they heard the voice of the sculptor belting out Methodist hymns.

Like most of his other experiences with architectural sculpture, the Time-Life Screen was a disappointment to Moore. To begin with, the London County Council frightened itself into thinking that if the stones were moved, one of them might fall onto a crowded pavement below. The stones were required to remain stationary, and Moore's good idea went for nothing. Then the building itself is undistinguished, and drags the sculpture down with it, making it look merely decorative —an attempt to save a bad cake with good frosting. Inside the lobby, as if in confirmation of the failure of the stone Screen, is the bronze working model—an altogether happier piece of sculpture. Moore would dearly like to buy the stone Screen back from Time-Life, and set it up in his own grounds.

In 1952–1953 he modeled and cast what is probably his most popular sculpture—not among artists but the gallery-going public—the bronze King and Queen. Two thin figures sit next to each other on a bench, their legs draped, their hands and feet articulated. Their bodies are wide pieces of bronze, slightly bent and humanized. But the King's head is the purest invention. Part head and part crown, part beard and part face, it is another thin piece of metal set at right angles to the thinness of the body. A single hole gives the King two eyes, and the Queen's head is a diminishment of the King's. The couple is archaic and archetypal, representing the permanent human residue of ancient memories of royalty.

In the years since he made the first maquette, Moore has thought of two sources for the King and Queen; he was aware of neither at the time. When Mary was little, Moore read fairy stories to her every day. His imagination was touched by a multitude of kings and queens, princes and peasants' daughters. Then there was also, typically, a memory from the British Museum: In the Egyptian rooms there are a number of carvings of a priest and his wife sitting side by side. An Egyptian Limestone Seated Figure is the sculpture Moore remembers especially. The official and his wife are rocky and solid—their carver was not playing with space or with thin forms—but something still and ritual in their side-by-side posture, which Moore makes royal, helped to make up the King and Queen.

The King's head was the first thing that happened. Moore was idly fingering a piece of wax, with no idea of making such an image. He pinched the wax between thumb and forefinger, and the result made

At Dumfries

him think of the god Pan—or of a king. In a few minutes he virtually completed the head. Later the same day he made the King's body. He dropped a flat sheet of wax in a pan of water to soften it, and cut it with a knife, and bent and rolled it to its proper thin shape.

The idea of the couple crystallized overnight. "The formal thing, then, became how thin I could make it. One meant it to be as spatial as any group sculpture could be." The next day he made the bench and a Queen to sit on it, space between her and the King. He added a thin wire-like frame, squaring the couple on all sides, and the maquette was finished. A copy was cast from the wax, and then subsequent bronzes based on the first bronze. Moore keeps the first one, which he thinks is the best: It retains the sharp edge the knife left in the wax. When he plays ping-pong near the maquette, there is a special house rule: The player who hits the ball into the Queen's lap wins game, set and match.

When he modeled the large version, he had to make several changes. He tried using the frame but it looked too much like a soccer goal. The hands and feet, which are lumps in the maquette, in the large sculpture are articulated into fingers and toes. It is here that some critics find that the big version fails. (They prefer the maquette.) They find an inexcusable formal disparity between the invention of the heads and the realism of the hands and feet. Moore doesn't agree. The large version, he says, allowed him to carry further the human implications of the King and Queen. Working over it, he felt that he could add meaning, or slant meaning, by how he made the hands. The King's hand resting on his knee could be clenched like a dictator's, or floppy like a weak king's, or in between. He used his details psychologically, thinking of the Queen as prim, upright, proper, while the King is "so sure of authority that he *can* relax, yet the head is alert." Also, "I see nothing wrong in the disparity of styles. Nobody minds that some figures in Chartres Cathedral are realistic heads on top of columns. In every work of art, some parts are more worked out than others." One should add that disparity (of size and of style) is an old habit of Moore's; there was the Life Drawing of 1928, with its realistic head and sculptural body, and the 1931 Mother and Child with its contrast of head and shoulders.

At the same time he was doing the King and Queen, with its mixture of myth and realism, he did the classical Draped Reclining Figure for the Time-Life terrace, and the abstracted series of internal and external forms executed from 1952 to 1954. Sculpture in two pieces, one inside the other, had been part of his repertoire since the helmet heads of 1940, but the combination of reclining figure and mother with child never occurred until the Cranbrook Reclining Figure of 1945–1946. Here the internal piece is not literally separated from the external, but is a swelling inside the opened-up reclining woman. In the words of the psychoanalytical critic quoted earlier, it is "both slug and foetus."

In the bronze and elm versions of the upright internal and external forms—the elm is at the Albright Gallery in Buffalo—the internal form, with a large hole for an eye, stands up in the darkness of its shelter, balancing with its piercing quality the inclusive organic external form. There are bronzes of the small version of the reclining figure (internal and external forms), an alert inner part sticking its neck up through the face-hole of the outer part. (All of these figures make one creature at the same time that they make two; it is part of their variety.) But when Moore finished the large version, he decided to leave out the inside piece, and so made the one-piece Reclining Figure (internal and external forms) of 1953–1954. The curving, female hollowness draws us inside.

Also in these years the British Council was exhibiting new Moores and old in Brussels, Paris, Amsterdam, Hamburg, Dusseldorf, and Berne. In 1951 they showed him in Athens, and he went there for the first time, his eyes open: "The Parthenon right now is probably much more impressive than when it was first made. You feel the spaces much more, and the openings, and the fact that it's not solid throughout and that the light comes in makes it into a piece of sculpture. . . . The Greek landscape was another revelation to me . . . that stark, stony quality, with the feeling that the sea may be round the next corner. I can understand why they were sculptors—the stone just had to be used." The Greeks were equally impressed by Henry Moore, or ΧΕΝΡΥ ΜΟΥΡ, as the cover of the catalogue put it. The British Council tries to fly him to the opening of its exhibitions whether he speaks the language or not, because he seems to be an effective ambassador just standing there and smiling. People mob him as if he were a pop singer. In Athens they broke windows to see him, and thirty-four thousand people attended the two-week exhibition.

Later an exhibition toured six Scandinavian cities, and went back to eight more galleries in Germany, and then was seen by thirty-five thousand Yugoslavs. Poland came later, and Portugal and Spain, and more German cities. (Public ownership generally correlates with the density of British Council exhibitions. German city-states now vie with each other in owning Moores.) Things were happening in the United States too. After one show Valentin wrote him, "You'll be glad to hear that you are getting more and more popular, to the extent that during the last two months, three of your small bronzes were stolen from the gallery. Congratulations." In 1951 Valentin showed thirty-four sculptures and thirty drawings, and he planned a second large exhibition for late 1954. Moore and Valentin had become close. For six years Valentin spent Christmas with the Moores at Hoglands, and they met every summer as well. After Christmas, 1953, Valentin became seriously ill. His artists were worried. "It's your holy duty to be very careful with your life," Kokoschka wrote him. "I would not like to face a future without you." In August Valentin stayed in Italy with Marino Marini while the sculptor did a portrait bust of him. On the morning of the 19th, during a sitting, clay fell from the armature on one side of the face. Marini was terrified and stopped the sitting, saying that something bad was going to happen. Later in the day Valentin died of an embolism.

Moore wrote a letter to Valentin's chief assistant in New York. "He treated his gallery as an artist should his work. . . . He sold only the work of artists he believed in. . . . To try to work out why one loved him so much is not easy. He was naturally shy and never demonstrative. How much, all this time, one unconsciously counted on his steadfast support, on him being there, tirelessly working for the cause of the painters and sculptors he believed in. I loved him very deeply and shall miss him terribly." The Rodin statue of Balzac in the garden of the Museum of Modern Art was presented in memory of Curt Valentin by his friends. Moore dedicated the catalogue of his 1962 Knoedler show to him.

The gallery went ahead with its large exhibition of Moore later in 1954, the last show Valentin had planned. There were thirty-two sculptures, including a king and queen. The real estate firm of Uris bought the King and Queen and installed it in the lobby of a new building. A tenant who rented a number of floors did not approve: either the King and Queen went, or he went. The King and Queen

went. Valentin's estate bought it back and sold it to the collector Joseph Hirshhorn. Then in 1955 Valentin's gallery broke up, and Knoedler's became Moore's New York dealers. Now through a nearly undecipherable series of events, Moore is shown in New York by Knoedler's *and* Marlborough-Gerson; in London by Leicester *and* Marlborough.

Curt Valentin has no successor in Moore's life, but Harry Fischer of Marlborough Galleries is the closest thing to it. Fischer tends to him, gets theater tickets for him, and travels abroad with him. Moore is not under contract to him or to anybody else. "Henry is a typical Yorkshireman," says Fischer. "You can only work with him if you give him complete freedom. Tie him down and you lose him." One of the unspoken reasons for the lack of a contract is that Moore wants to be able to deal with his friends himself. His best and oldest friends have magnificent Moore collections, acquired usually not as gifts but as sales at low prices. At least one of them is poor enough to have trouble paying insurance on his collection.

Reclining Figure
(external form), 1953–1954

Internal and External Forms,
1953–1954

Moore was slow to raise his prices. Modern art in England tripled in price between 1952 and 1960 (after an auction of E. C. Gregory's estate at Sotheby's in 1959, dealers rushed to their showrooms and doubled the prices of all their English artists) and Moore sometimes lagged far enough behind the market to become attractive to mere speculators. He has kept his editions of bronzes smaller than many

135

artists, and has avoided a revision of his tax status which could save him sixty thousand pounds a year, because he does not think it would be right. He finds himself rich enough: He drives a Rover, and he bought the farm next door in 1956 and built new studios. He is generous to his friends, and at the same time many of his friends point to small touches of stinginess in him, which make no sense in his present situation, but which perhaps survive from years of having to be careful about money. Opinion has it that his assistants are underpaid.

Moore still shows at Leicester on occasion (and Gimpel Fils some-times buys and shows the odd Moore) but most of his work goes to Marlborough. Probably he grew less happy with Leicester Galleries as his work got bigger. Leicester never gave him more than one room for a show, and when the Dartington Hall Reclining Figure was shown together with the elm Reclining Figure of 1945–1946, visitors felt massive claustrophobia when they walked in, and couldn't see either of them properly. But for that matter, the relationship of an artist to most of his dealers is bound to have some irony to it. Moore tells a true story about two gallery-owners going to visit a dying artist. "How do you feel?" they asked him, standing on each side of his bed. "Like Christ— between two thieves," he answered.

From 1954 to 1956 Moore did the Warrior with Shield and the Falling Warrior, together with some of his original maquettes of the theme. The Falling Warrior's head is cleft open as if by an ax, an arm is cut off, and a leg is cut off at the knee; his body writhes with pain. It expresses a loathing and, like the King and Queen, translates it into a timeless image—here of a man struck and falling. The series began from a piece of flint which made him think of a gashed head; then he remembered the heads of animals in the open butcher shops of Castleford.

Also of the mid-fifties were the series of uprights culminating in the Glenkiln Cross (named for its most impressive site, the lonely part of Scotland where W. J. Keswick has placed it together with three other Moores). He had done uprights before: Some of the early upright stringed figures occurred to him as he worked on these; there were also the Three Standing Figures of 1945–1946 which are at Battersea, and the knobby surreal Upright Figure of 1950. These new forms began with one of Moore's semi-commissions. "In 1955 I was asked to consider making a sculpture for the courtyard of a new building in Milan. I visited the site and a lone Lombardy poplar growing behind the building convinced one that a vertical work would act as the correct counterfoil to the horizontal rhythm of the building." He did ten variations, and at first there was too much of the Ethnographic room of the British Museum. "I started by balancing different forms one above the other—with results rather like the Northwest American totem poles—but as I continued the attempts gained more unity, also became perhaps more organic—and then one in particular . . . took on the shape of a crucifix—a kind of worn-down body and a cross merged into one."

Moore didn't plan to make a cross; as with the King's head, his fingers did the thinking. "Straightaway it was a cross, the symbol took over." When he made the Glenkiln Cross full size, he scratched ladder marks on the front of it. He turned five of the maquettes into large sculptures, and "three of them grouped themselves together, and in my mind, assumed the aspect of a crucifixion scene as though framed against the sky above Golgotha." Since the Glenkiln Cross meant more than the other uprights, it was made larger and central. The Glenkiln stands by itself in Scotland, as some of the others do elsewhere, but Moore likes them best as a trio—essentially a three-part sculpture. That some of them stand singly is a result of their price. The Amon Carter Museum at Forth Worth paid $100,000 for its set of three; there is another set at the Kröller-Müller Museum in Holland. But none of them is at Olivetti, the building in Milan. The Glenkiln Cross became too religious, Moore felt, to stand in front of a commercial building. Then he discovered that the sculpture courtyard was also being used as a carpark. The uprights would most of the day have been cut off halfway up. One sees why Moore prefers elastic commissions.

Would-be commissions are constantly coming to him. The attention is gratifying, no doubt, but it can be a bother. In the thirties the Hampstead artists were despised by press and Establishment. But how does John Cage feel when Henry Pleasants starts praising him? From the time of the shelter drawings Moore has been praised by the idiots as well as the people who knew and understood. It is a special kind of loneliness for the contemporary artist to be so fashionable among the Philistines that their praise isolates him from his peers. There is also the well-known loneliness of fame, that human law which makes it all but impossible for old friends to remain intimate when one of them is

The making of the Warrior
with Shield

accorded international celebrity, and the other is not. His old Castleford
friends remember him as Buck or Hal. London friends in the twenties
and thirties called him Harry. Most of the friends he sees now call
him Henry, and carry a Sir in front of their names, not for their ancestors but for their accomplishments.

Moore turned down the offer of a knighthood late in the fifties. (He
was made Companion of Honour in 1955, and received the Order of
Merit in 1962, and so has become Henry Moore, O.M., C.H. The O.M.
is considerably more distinguished than a knighthood; only twenty-
four men at any time can wear the Order.) He never took seriously the
possibility of accepting it; he realized that if the day started with his

assistants saying, "Good morning, Sir Henry," he wouldn't be able to work at all.

Moore's honors have won him audiences with Her Majesty Queen Elizabeth II, whose appreciation of art is rumored to be limited to paintings of horses. On the occasion of the C.H., Moore and Her Majesty discussed the monument to her father which had recently passed the Royal Fine Art Commission, of which Moore is a member. Moore and Prince Philip spoke about the Hyde Park Quadriga, a sculptural object including horses, which is visible from Buckingham Palace.

The Royal Fine Art Commission is only one of Moore's committees.

He was a trustee of the Tate Gallery for two terms of seven years each. (Second terms are unusual.) He is a trustee of the National Gallery, a member of the Arts Council, and on the board of the National Theater. He does not always do his homework for meetings, but he is invaluable in the discussion of a problem. "Henry's very strong in the head, you know," says one of his chairmen. "Any problem you bring to Henry, he brings a clear and strong mind to it." But the idea of the great sculptor serving on committees offends many of his admirers. Even some of his chairmen object to his service on *other* committees. Partly he does it because he finds it hard to say no, partly because he is a socialist who believes in state patronage, and partly because he is gregarious: He likes talk, even if it follows an agenda.

Of course the honors, the committees and the titled friends bring Moore into the Establishment too. English society has a genius for accommodating rebels. It may attack Moore for twenty years; then for the next twenty it will cover him with praises. Moore won't join the Royal Academy, and didn't accept the knighthood, but it would be only pique if he insisted on disowning totally the Establishment which had disowned him once. The Tate, which once wouldn't show him at any cost, now has the best collection of Moore in England. Sir John Rothenstein took over the directorship in 1938, and collected Moore as soon as he was able. Moore assisted (tracing down old carvings, getting permission from owners to cast one more bronze of an edition) instead of exercising his pride and staying out.

Naturally he does not lack detractors from the left, as he used to have them from the right. The absolute eminence attributed to Moore, by people who are not students of sculpture, irritates critics and sculptors who are used to finer distinctions, and who know that some Moores are better than others. Some detraction is considerably stronger. Immediately after the war, at the time of the New York and Venice triumphs, reactions among the young were probably the strongest they have ever been; they used Giacometti and Gonzalez as sticks to beat Moore with. Later the intensity diminished, but the reactions continue, as they must. One young sculptor calls him academic not because he resembles the Royal Academy but because he has made an academy of himself; he just takes bones and pebbles and fabricates form from them, "like a sculpture factory." A painter is critical of his repeated themes: "If he does any more of those earth

141

Three Upright Figures, 1955–1956

mothers, I'll throw up." Another young sculptor finds him antique, old-fashioned and romantic, an antediluvian figure out of the far reaches of history on the other side of the Great War. Moore reminds him of Elgar as opposed to Stravinsky: Moore is "old English landscape and full of God and all that."

Most violent of the attackers now are a few of the younger sculptors. Doubtless some of them are merely jealous, but there are reasons more urgent than jealousy. It is imperative, if one wishes to become a good artist, not to be drawn into the gravitational field of a master. There was even this joke: "Knock, knock." "Who's there?" "Henry Moore." "Henry Moore who?" "Are there Henry Moore at home like you?" The answer, from late in the twenties for thirty years, was a distinct affirmative. Bernard Meadows fought to ward off the influence, and so did many others, but most of them remained satellites. English sculpture existed more honestly than it had done since the middle ages, but the presence of a master was a limitation to his school. (Blank verse languished as long as it was Shakespearian, and later as long as it was Miltonic.) Anthony Caro, another former assistant to Moore, about a decade younger than Meadows, is a pivotal figure in contemporary English sculpture. He is surely one of the best young sculptors anywhere. His work began within Moore-ish premises of organic form, and later became expressionist and more like Dubuffet. Then abruptly in 1959, after a visit to the United States, Caro began to work in assembled metal stretched out in bizarre linkages from which the sense of touch was effectively removed. Both technique and material are antipathetic to Moore's sculptural premises, and create a useful alternative direction. In an interview Caro even said that he wouldn't work outside, and that these huge forms belong indoors. Curiously some of his steel assemblages sprawl in the attitude of a reclining figure.

A group of Caro's students at St. Martin's School of Art—Philip King and William Tucker especially—work in materials like plastic, and with considerable attention paid to color but little to volume. Another prominent opposite to Moore is a Scot named Eduardo Paolozzi, who makes violent constructions out of machinery, ultimately in the direction of automata. Recent English shows of young art students are dominated by gaudy fantasies in molded plastic. Some of the young seem to be saying the name of Henry Moore backwards, Eroom Yrneh, in order to avoid the stigma of imitation—another irrational aesthetic, hopefully as effective as the earlier irrational apotheosis of carving.

Toward the end of the fifties anti-Moore forces—especially a few critics at that time—gained ground in the weekly and Sunday papers, the English no man's land of reputations. People began to wonder if Moore's smooth path from obscurity to fame would be climaxed by a decline into the passé. Moore himself, some friends observed, was aware of the movement to dump him, and unhappy about it. Then abruptly he survived his attackers. The voices against him are heard in studios but seldom in public. Perhaps the great bronzes of the end of the decade, beginning with the Glenkiln Cross, are responsible. But

The Rondanini Pietà

more likely the public reaction is purely irrelevant to any judgment of artistic merit. One of his chief detractors, foiled in an attempt to take over the Tate, retreated to France. The history of reputations (a study separate from the history of art, but not wholly separate) thrives on lesser events.

Moore always has dreaded the possibility of slipping, not in reputation but in ability and taste. In France one time he feared going to Vence, afraid that Matisse's chapel would be slack and only a monument of the vogue for painting chapels. When he saw it he was moved by Matisse's enduring integrity. As ever, Moore's model is Michelangelo. His favorite Michelangelo carving is the Rondanini Pietà, which stands in the Castello Sforzesco. Michelangelo started work on it about ten years before his death, and probably finished it then in a smooth style. But just before he died, in 1564, he cut off the top of the old statue and recarved most of the rest of it, leaving the legs and a nearly detached arm of the older work. Moore told David Sylvester in 1964, on the four-hundredth anniversary of Michelangelo's death, that perhaps Michelangelo "knew he was near death and his values were more spiritual than they had been." He finds in this sculpture a "quality you get in the work of old men who are really great. They can simplify; they can leave out . . . their late works become simplified and fragmentary, become imperfect and unfinished. The artists stop caring about beauty and such abstract ideas, and yet their works get greater."

He was nearly sixty-six when he spoke, and he was expressing his hope that he would improve as he matured; Michelangelo lived to be eighty-nine. Two premises sustain him, in his continuing effort: "The less time one has left in life, the less does one want to distract or disperse one's energies," and "the more you think about form, and the understanding of form, and about human nature, the more you agree with Michelangelo that sculpture can do anything." But only if you are very demanding of yourself. Moore himself moves and changes, within his work, by dissatisfaction with past work. From 1956 to 1958 he modeled two large sculptures called Seated Woman and Woman. The first woman is exaggerated in her womanly pregnancy, but complete with arms, hands and head. When Moore had finished it, he was dissatisfied; it was too anecdotal, it dispersed its power. He made the second all torso, with enormous female rhythms of breast and womb and buttocks, and no head or arms. Here are the power and the feeling.

Seated Woman, 1957

Woman, 1957–1958

8

1958–1965:
The Lincoln Center
Reclining Figure

N 1958 Moore completed his bigger sculpture, the sixteen-foot, twenty-ton, marble Reclining Figure for the UNESCO building in Paris. Moore took a commission this time. but was free to do whatever he wished. When he was trying to find the right idea, he was nervous, and his voice grew hoarse and nearly left him. (The same symptoms returned five years later, when he was planning his even larger Lincoln Center piece.) He was anxious that the UNESCO piece be a major work, because of its size and its public position. The figure—which was carved in two pieces at the Henraux quarries in Italy, largely by assistants—is a composite Henry Moore, almost an *average* Henry Moore reclining figure. Looking at the UNESCO piece, one remembers the critic who prefers Giacometti to Moore because, "Moore does not risk all by moving into the area of total uncertainty." In making it, Moore worked within his own achievements and certainties. Yet the result, though a breakthrough in nothing but size, has the virtues of a Henry Moore work—a massive stony presence that is considerably older than the streets among which it sits.

The UNESCO piece had to be large, to cope with the buildings around it. Probably the challenge of its size is one of the reasons Moore accepted the commission. Early Moores were small not on principle but because Moore couldn't afford big pieces of stone or wood, and because it was difficult to get large pieces into small studios. As soon as he was able to work outside on holidays in Kent, his major pieces grew in size. Working outside helped him be hard on himself, too. "Always in any studio there is a place where things look better, where their less good views can be turned to the wall, and where the lighting suits them. . . ." But when you carve outside, "Surface scratchings won't show in dull English weather. Only big architectural contrasts of masses—real sculptural power, real sculptural organization—will tell at all on a dull day."

Moore likes his sculpture to stand permanently out in nature, too, and to be big enough to take the comparison its natural forms invite. For a while modernist sculpture was typically an indoor art (the parks were left to academic equestrians) but now the London County Council has an outdoor exhibition every three years at Battersea Park; and there are regular outdoor shows at Middleheim Park in Belgium, at Sonsbeek in Holland, and all over Europe and Latin America. There are also a growing number of permanent outdoor sculpture parks. His own sculpture park in Hertfordshire is not ideal, but "only a *setting* for things, because there are no roughnesses. . . . I often long for a bit of hill that can put things against the sky." The ideal place is the bare Scottish estate where four sculptures reside "in a landscape which is, I should say, exactly as it was thirty million years ago."

Huge pieces make problems. He has to question whether the crane will be able to get up the drive. But he has never troubled about such crises. A neighbor who was astonished at his practicality kept marveling until Moore finally answered, more shortly than usual, "Anyone who can't manage the practical side of his life is a fool." In Hampstead curving iron steps to his studio were his trouble, not cranes in drives. Then it was a major triumph against natural obstacles to carve a reclining figure four feet by two feet. The Lincoln Center piece is twenty-eight by seventeen. He is delighted by the sheer size of it. Small pieces look like toys to him now.

Yet looking through photographs of Moore's early work, one imagines that the sculptures are large. A reclining woman sprawls and looms; she looks ten feet long and five feet high; but the printed

The UNESCO Reclining Figure, 1957–1958

Moore and the Venus

At Stonehenge

dimensions are inches not feet. The rocky Mother and Child of 1922 is only eleven inches high; the 1925 Mother and Child (the child over the mother's head) stands twenty-two and a half inches. Even the 1929 Reclining Figure is only thirty-three inches long. Probably to the uninitiated eye the photographs are more impressive than the carvings. But to Moore the effect of monumentality is the whole point. Size allows sculpture to compete with nature and provides new problems to solve, but without monumentality size is nothing, and with monumentality the small takes on the emotional scale of the huge. Monumentality is not a property of sculpture only. Moore admires it in his favorite painters: "The little sketches of horses that Leonardo made in his sketchbook were sometimes no bigger than a thumbnail, but you don't have that idea when you look at them. You think of a horse big enough to make a statue. And the same with Michelangelo sketches.

There's a mental scale independent of the actual physical scale. . . . There are some things like, for example, the Albert Memorial, that are really just enlarged small ideas; they are wrong in their scale; they haven't got their true physical size."

While Moore has concentrated on modeling large sculptures, his drawing has almost stopped. "Sculpture . . . gives me nearly all that I want to do," he says. "When one is young there are lots of possibilities that one hasn't tried out; drawing is a means of finding your ways about things, and a way of experiencing, more quickly than sculpture allows, certain tryouts and attempts." When he was young he could not afford to cast maquettes, and carving took too long to be used as a means of sketching, and clay or plasticine is not durable. In order to test a variety of ideas he used drawing; now he is able to model, cast what he likes, and keep it to look at. His sketches are three-dimensional now, which may lead to a greater three-dimensionality in his large pieces.

As he grows older, everything tends to concentrate on sculpture. He reads less then he used to (he will read almost anything about Michelangelo, and tried to read Irving Stone's *The Agony and the Ecstasy*, but couldn't swallow it), and sees fewer people. Socially, the Moores see the couple across the street perhaps once a month, and the family doctor three or four evenings a year, and more rarely a few other local people. Old friends occasionally drive out from London for a drink in the late afternoon. A portion of each year goes to travel. Some of it is work: He visits a quarry in Italy, or a sculpture site in Germany, or opens an exhibition in Brazil. Once he made an unpleasant trip to Auschwitz to judge a competition for a monument to be erected there; he loathed the place, and the sense that its loathsomeness was being used, and himself used too. Occasionally the travel is a weekend with friends; to stay with the Ashes on their estate in Devon, where the river Dart winds around the house; or to visit the Constantine Fitzgibbons in Dorset. In their garden the Fitzgibbons kept a plaster cast of the Venus de Milo, remnant of a defunct art school. Marian Fitzgibbon revealed to Irina Moore that the Venus had a hole in her head; do you suppose Henry would mind fixing it? "Henery will *love* it!" He threw himself into the task with ebullience. The Fitzgibbons had some rather passé plaster which Moore mixed in a pudding basin—all the time lecturing them on the necessity of freshness to plaster—and climbed the ladder and painstakingly, with great dignity, refinished the Venus de Milo. There are photographs of the operation, which look like an attempt at blackmail: Henry Moore in his checked coat bends seriously to work on his latest sculpture.

The Moores often take their annual summer holiday with friends. In the thirties they went somewhere with the Coxons, or the Nicholsons, or the Ivon Hitchenses. At first they visited English resorts: Sizewell in Suffolk, Broadstairs in Kent. Recently they have tended to go to Italy, and they traveled as far as Yugoslavia in 1963. (The two-week Yugoslavian trip was the longest leave Moore had ever taken from work.) On the road and in the restaurants, Moore relaxes and entertains; he loves the good food of France and Italy. But when he goes into a museum he is serious, and a harsh critic. He disapproves of a Delacroix because "the arm doesn't come out properly"; and he finds a particular Ingres repulsive. He detests the busy and loves the monumental. (One of his favorite paintings is Gordale Scar by James Ward, a vigorous Yorkshire landscape which hangs in the Tate.) He and a friend went to the Rijksmuseum in Amsterdam because Moore wanted to revisit a Rembrandt. He walked directly to The Anatomy Lesson, looking neither left nor right ("If you go to a gallery, never look at more than one or two pictures") and sat in front of it for an hour and a half.

There are also the social occasions in London—a first night at the National Theater, a reception for Joseph Hirshhorn who *might* be persuaded to leave his collection to England since New York won't build a museum for it in Central Park, or an opening of an exhibition. A few years ago, his phone rang and he was told that Prime Minister Nehru was in town, and would like to meet him. He refused, because he and Irina were visiting Mary at school that day; then he thought, No, *Mary* would like to meet Nehru; let's accept. When Igor Stravinsky came to London in 1962, he wanted to meet Henry Moore, so Stephen Spender had them to dinner at his house. The two men took to each other, and at the end of the dinner Stravinsky asked Moore if he could buy a drawing. Moore said he'd like to give him one, but it was too late to drive out to Perry Green. Spender offered to give Stravinsky his pick of Spender's own Moore drawings, and Moore said he would give Spender two drawings for the one Stravinsky chose. Stravinsky picked a shelter-period drawing in several panels. A few weeks later, when

Spender visited Hoglands, Moore was embarrassed that he had no drawings fit to trade. The best Moore drawings in the house belong to Irina, and Henry will not take them back. So Moore gave Spender a green bronze three-quarter figure instead of two drawings. Stravinsky sent each of them an autograph page of music.

In 1963 Moore received the Italian Feltrinelli prize, a sort of Nobel for artists, worth about $42,000. Moore immediately wondered if it was taxable, and telephoned T. S. Eliot—the only friend (and fellow O.M.) he could think of who had won a Nobel—to ask if the Nobel was taxable. It was not, nor is the Feltrinelli. Moore went to Italy with Irina, and received the award from Signor Segni, the President of Italy. He was greatly pleased and honored, but friends report with amusement that he was *more* pleased and *more* honored when he was made a Freeman of Castleford the year before. Irina blessed the occasion by wearing a hat, which she is loath to do. The Worshipful Mayor of Castleford, Alderman Jack Smart J.P., presented the Honorary Freedom of the Borough to Mr. Henry Moore C.H. Moore's citation ended: "In recognition and appreciation of the great contribution which he has made to the enjoyment of art and sculpture the world over, and to his great achievements and the world-wide fame which has attended them, remembering with particular pride and joy that he was born in Castleford, the son of a miner, and spent his early life in the town. . . ." If he really was more excited by the Castleford occasion, it is not entirely surprising. The Italian prize went to the public figure, which is separate from the man in the far room handling a piece of wax. But inside any artist of sixty there is always the *wunderkind* who decided to become a great sculptor. The people one set out to astonish were not Italian presidents or Indian prime ministers or Russian émigré composers, but neighbors in the rows of identical houses.

In the late fifties he started the series of sculptures in two parts which culminated in the Lincoln Center piece of 1963–1964. In 1959, when he was making the first of them full-size, he said, "I am obsessed with the idea of making a reclining figure out of two pieces which will be related to each other but separate; one end is the leg part of the sculpture and the other end is the head and body part. But between them I am trying to make a kind of mixture of the human figure and of landscape.

"One might even use a composite of three pieces. Might even turn to four. . . . I first did some sculpture in four pieces in 1933, I think, or 1934. The new pieces aren't a conscious turning back, but I suppose when you've done a work which has meant something special to you, you are liable to use that experience again."

Among the early series is the Pynkado wood Two Forms of 1934. "I remember making it, very vividly. The pieces were in a mother and child relationship, although the two forms were entirely separate. I think some of the other several-piece sculptures [of the thirties] came about because it was easier to experiment with the problem of space by moving one form a certain distance away from another, and this distance could easily be changed, giving a freer chance to experiment with the spaces between forms."

The separation of parts of a body—where the pieces added up to a reclining figure, for instance—was a development of the Hole, a further opening-up of space within commonly solid forms.

"In doing the present series," Moore said in 1959, "it came naturally and without any conscious decision, that I made it in two pieces. After a time, I began to realize that I was simplifying something of the essential elements of my reclining figure theme. In most of my reclining figures the head and neck part of the sculpture, sometimes the torso part too, is usually upright, which gives a contrast to the horizontal rhythm of the whole sculpture. Also I, very often, have made a sort of looming leg—the top leg in the sculpture projecting over the lower leg, which gives a sense of thrust or power, as a large branch of a tree might move outwards from the main trunk or as a seaside cliff might overhang from below, if you are on the beach." His remarks foreshadow the Lincoln Center piece as clearly as they recall the Leeds Reclining Figure of 1929.

The relationship of two parts allows him to achieve again the monumentality of disproportion, and it also allows him to treat the two parts of one woman as a mother and child. Eventually Moore was to expand to three pieces, as in his Three-Part Reclining Figure of 1961–1962, where the sculpture is both a single woman and a family group. He was to use the two-part structure for pieces leaning on each other—the sense of leaning quite kinesthetic—in the Bridge Figure of 1964. Other two-parts left the reclining figure behind, and became a new series of abstracted heads, like the 1962 Knife-Edge (Two-Piece) and the Locking Piece.

155

Two-Piece Reclining Figure No. 1, 1959

Two-Piece Reclining Figure No. 2, 1960

But at the beginning of the series he made four large bronze reclining figures—one in 1959, another in 1960, and two in 1961. In the first, the leg looms like a hollowed-out cliff, and its massiveness hangs in the air with a sense of arrested motion. In the second, the leg part settles into its base like a sheer cliff, precisely *un*hollowable. All of these sculptures express the female and the earthy, and at the same time include great variety of reference. Moore has never made another group of sculptures which so completely fulfill his desire for three-dimensionality. Though they are massive and monumental, as you walk around them they open up and lighten at certain angles, apparently changing their shape utterly. Here is a torso carved out of space, here is a mountain, here is a Cycladic profile.

One of the sources of this group, as he mentions, was the multiple-part series of the thirties. But really only the basic idea of part sculpture, which Moore found in Arp, connected the two sets. The only

Two-Piece Reclining Figure No. 5, 1963

Monet:
Cliff at Étretat

Adel Crag

Seurat:
Le Bec du Hoc

artistic sources of the second series are paintings by Monet and Seurat: The Monet paintings of the cliffs at Étretat, where the illusion of rockiness is enhanced by holes worn through the rocks, the sea shining beyond them; and the Seurat Le Bec du Hoc, which resembles the foot part only. The strangest and most potent source of the two-parts is not artistic at all. When Moore was a boy in Castleford, perhaps ten years old, he and his family visited the town of Adel (pronounced addle) a few miles away. They picnicked on Adel Moor, a patch of wild, rocky land a mile from the village center. All Moore remembers now, of his

hours there, is a large rock, and he is not so sure he remembers that. He wonders if his memory has tricked him—not having seen it in more than fifty years—because he remembers it as huge, like the mountainous slag heaps of Castleford. "Maybe it's no bigger than this room."

If you go to Adel Moor now, you do not see the big stone at first. In the scrubby woods are a number of small boulders surfaced with ripples, a fragile effect which looks remarkably like Moore's drapery. Also, a light green moss turns the stone the color of one of Moore's patinas. When you move more deeply into the tangled wood, you come to what local people call Adel Crag. You realize at once why Moore remembers and distrusts the memory: It is an enormous two-part reclining figure which Moore must have made between 1959 and 1965. It does not resemble earlier reclining figures or two-parts. One or another of its features turns up in all the members of the recent series. Of the two huge rocks which make up the crag, one is narrow and vertical; the other is split, enormous and jagged, and provides head and torso while the vertical piece is the raised looming knees. It is about thirty feet long, and eighteen feet high—even larger than the Lincoln Center piece. The depth of the Millstone Grit rock is constant but the crag is sited on a slope, so that knees are higher than head, helping to create monumentality. Around it grow silver birch and bracken, and there are gray stone walls at the near border of Adel Moor, with the same green moss softening the stone. At the knees' end of the rock is an old oak, the roots built up on the ground and busy with fingers and limbs.

During the years of the two-parts, Moore was doing other forms as well. He has always found it necessary, and stimulating, to work on different things at once. It allows him to do more work; when he is tired of one set of problems, another may wake him up. His upright elmwood figure at the Guggenheim Museum is dated 1956–1960, and the four years represent necessity. The carving is nearly ten feet tall, and the original elm trunk weighed two tons (about a quarter is carved away). The wood dried at the rate of about two inches a year, and if he had cut faster than it dried, he would have risked cracks in the wood which would spoil his ideas. It took him a long time to find a good elm trunk, and when he found one he found another almost immediately. So he also carved the elmwood Reclining Figure, 1959–1964. Originally he planned it for the Tate, which had long wanted a large wooden sculpture, but by the time he finished he decided he would keep it himself—he hadn't had one either.

One other theme particularly occupied him at this time, as well as the two-parts. He was exploring the formal use of the sharp edge. His early work was blunt and stony. When he did tubular lead figures in the late thirties, he kept the edges smooth. The first sharp objects are pieces from cut wax, like some parts of the rocking-chair figures, and the King and Queen. But the large King and Queen explores thinness, not sharpness. Late in the fifties he became interested in the sharpness of certain pieces of bone. The Bone Figure (Knife-Edge) bronze of 1961 was the most direct result. This upright figure, which is unquestionably female, stood atop a small hill near the entrance to the Battersea Park outdoor sculpture exhibition of 1963. Her torso is an immense, thin piece of bone, broken off jaggedly at one edge, the way bone breaks. The plane inclines at the back—a sort of bustle—and veers off abruptly. The head is a thin repetition and simplification of the torso. The figure has grace and dignity, and is also a *memento mori*. No one can deny the expressiveness of knife and bone.

In 1962 Moore cast the twenty-inch version of the Knife-Edge (Two-Piece). This sculpture and the Locking Piece of the same year are heads which are as little representative as anything in Moore's work. The Knife-Edge is the first coincidence of the two-part theme and the theme of sharpness. When one sees the two pieces of Knife-Edge from the thin side, it is space sculpture almost entirely; from any of the uncountable angles at which the two pieces overlap, the bronze configures a variety of associations. On some of its sides the sculpture is sharp enough to cut.

Moore's major effort of this decade, the Lincoln Center Reclining Figure, began December 17, 1961, when Frank Stanton of CBS, who is a Director of Lincoln Center, visited Moore in Much Hadham. He suggested that Moore do something for the pool in the North Plaza, and spread the architect's plans on the floor of Moore's living room. "By George," Moore exclaimed, "it's as big as a cricket pitch." Moore was intrigued, largely because he would have a chance to make something coming out of water like Monet. The watery base was his fascination. "You must be able to *think* that it goes down to a bottom, like rocks." When he had finished the plaster of the full-size sculpture, he threw buckets of water over the zinc-covered platform on which it stood, to see how it looked in reflection.

He was not tempted to do anything symbolic of the site—images of the performing arts or whatever—because, as he says, he had learned his lesson with the UNESCO piece; he had wasted a great deal of time trying to think out something related to UNESCO, before he substituted formal criteria. "I told them, when I saw pictures of the building and the poor, that I was interested in doing a two-part coming out of the water," simply that. They were interested too, but Moore as usual did not want a commission. He would do something that seemed suitable to him, and if they liked it they could have it.

Another reason Moore was intrigued was again the necessary size of the sculpture. "To stand up to the scale of the Plaza and surrounding

buildings," he wrote while he was still experimenting with alternatives, "it has to be even bigger than my UNESCO piece. . . . It turned out to be almost twice the size. "I like the challenge of working to a really large size—much bigger than I would be able to do if the work were just for myself, or just for exhibition."

Knife-Edge (Two-Piece), 1962

Standing Figure: Knife-Edge, 1961

In the summer of 1962 he made a series of small maquettes, all two-part reclining figures, in which he tried to cope with the problem of hugeness and the watery site. Two of them seemed better than the rest, but in their tiny size he found it impossible to choose between them. In the winter of 1962–1963, he modeled both of them half-size, fourteen feet. The winter of 1962–1963 was the worst Europe has suffered for a long time, and during portions of it the studios were too cold to work in. Moore retired to Hoglands and produced a series of lithographs, which he had promised to a publisher.

By the time he was fairly well along with the two fourteen-foot plasters, Moore felt he knew which one would be better. The other was not so good at rising out of the water. When both were done he painted them bronze-color and set them outside. He confirmed his choice, and was ready to start the large version. While he worked on the plaster of the Lincoln Center Reclining Figure, the rejected candidate stood on a platform outside his nearby studio. Eventually he will cast it in bronze, at its present fourteen-foot size.

There was never any question of using stone for the Lincoln Center piece, because of difficulties of transport and the severity of New York winters. It had to be modeled in plaster and cast in bronze, which created a number of practical problems. First of all, none of Moore's studios was large enough to house anything twenty-eight feet long and seventeen feet high, much less provide perspective on it. Moore needed a shelter for the sculpture, to keep rain off it and protect it during winter; at the same time he needed to be able to look at it from a distance, and from all angles. The final piece "must make its point at a considerable distance." He built a structure which looked like a transparent hangar for a small dirigible. It was constructed of slotted aluminum strips bolted together like an erector set, and covered with thick transparent plastic which could be rolled up in good weather. The hangar was near the new studios on a flat patch at the end of Moore's new land. He paced out the shape of the pool (the size of a tennis court) around it, and of the plaza itself (eighty-seven by eighty yards).

Moore's most experienced assistant, Robert Holding, worked on it together with Geoffrey Greetham. In the summer of 1963 they began the armature, tying the boards together with rope and hanging cheese-cloth from the extreme points of the wood. At first they did only the tallest part, the swooping torso, but after they had covered it with plaster, and it began to look like itself, it was necessary to start the foot part. Any changes or discriminations Moore might make depended on seeing the two together. He was extraordinarily careful, and mindful of the eventual site. "I've turned this sculpture the same angle to the sun that it will be in New York, so that I know that at eleven o'clock in the morning when I'm working on it, the sun will make more or less the same shadows, light and shade."

There were two crises before the end of the year. The assistants applied too much plaster to the top of the torso in relation to the strength of its base. Cracks appeared at the bending point, and Moore feared that the whole upper part might come crashing down. A heavy piece of timber shored it up. Then in December Moore panicked like an orange grower in a Florida frost. The temperature dropped abruptly and unseasonably, and there was no heat inside the dirigible hangar. Newly applied plaster is at least half water (drop dried plaster in a bucket of water and bubbles come up for hours) and if this water had frozen, the Lincoln Center Reclining Figure would have erupted, her skin shattering into thousands of pieces. Moore found a tarpaulin to hang over the one uncovered side of the structure, and bought a huge old tortoise stove to provide heat. It burned five hoppers of coke a night and the sculpture remained unfrozen and intact.

Moore let it alone for most of December and January—it was hard to work with the tarpaulin there, and the Locking Piece had to be finished for Brussels—but when the weather warmed up in February, work resumed with all intensity. As spring came he removed the tarpaulin, and even took out every other aluminum strut, in order to have a clearer view of the sculpture as he walked around it.

In a little construction next to the dirigible shed, the small version sat with its bronze paint covered with numbers showing distances from a movable frame of wood. Looking at the two pieces, one could not believe that they were in a ratio of two to one. The smaller one looked tiny. When the dimensions of a sculpture are doubled, its volume is increased eightfold. The viewer stays the same size while the sculpture grows, and this makes for changes. "I had to elongate the head and neck because the perspective from down below made them look shorter. I must have added a foot to what a precise copy would have been." It made Moore think of Pisano's figures for the top of the

Baptistry at Pisa, their necks tilted forward because of the angle at which they are seen. Size also meant that anyone close to the sculpture would not see it all at once; if you were close enough to see detail, you would have to carry your memory of one part with you when you looked at another. To Moore this was another problem to understand and solve.

On August 15, 1964, agents of Moore's Berlin founder, Hermann

Making the Lincoln Center Figure

Leaving Hoglands for Berlin

Noack (including Mr. Noack himself), arrived at Perry Green to begin the long process that would turn plaster into bronze. They took four days to saw the torso part into eleven pieces for transportation to Berlin, packing it carefully so that it would not crack as the Locking Piece had earlier in the year. A month later Moore and his assistants sawed up the foot part themselves, and sent it after its torso. In Berlin Noack cut the plaster into sixty-five small pieces for casting.

The delicate, perfectionist work of the founder took nearly a year, and Moore was able to turn to other things. He began the large copy of the Knife-Edge (Two-Piece), and finished an eleven-foot version of the Archer, which was displayed on a turntable at the Globe Theater on June 15, 1965, as part of a memorial to Moore's old friend T. S. Eliot. (The same program included music specially composed by Stravinsky, sets by Bridget Riley and readings of Eliot by Peter O'Toole, Sir Laurence Olivier and Groucho Marx.) But the biggest job after the Lincoln Center piece was the large Nuclear Energy, which Moore made

167

in the still-standing dirigible hangar. (Built as a temporary structure, it is unlikely ever to come down.)

Nuclear Energy, which was originally called the Atom Piece, began as another of Moore's recent group of heads, first a maquette and then a bronze about four feet high. While the intermediate size was being cast, he was approached by the University of Chicago to do a sculpture to stand on the site of the laboratory where Enrico Fermi made the first nuclear chain reaction, leading to the atomic bomb. Moore thought a moment, and then said that perhaps he had made the sculpture already. Chicago looked at the small version and agreed.

He had always intended to make a version twelve feet tall. As with the Locking Piece, the largest version is the best of the three. The four-foot bronze tends to remain a skull. In the large size the columnar lower half of the piece is released to take on its architectural identity, while the upper part widens out into a polished dome, at once skull and church dome and mushroom cloud.

In July, 1965, the Moores bought an Italian cottage in Forte dei Marmi, the village where the Italian sculptor Marino Marini lives, and spent most of August and the first part of September there. All three Moores love the sea-bathing there, which they discovered when Moore carved the UNESCO figure at the Henraux quarries two miles away. They plan to spend a portion of each summer in their primitive, two-room cottage; Moore plans to take a vacation by carving Henraux stone every summer (he started to carve a small version of the Archer for himself in 1965) and they will have the sunshine which the Hertfordshire August does not always supply.

In the meantime the Lincoln Center Reclining Figure was on the move. Noack welded the sixty-five separate pieces into the final two parts, removed the welding marks, and patinated the new-penny bronze a soft green. Then the founder packed the sculpture into two enormous crates, the metal covered with oiled paper to protect it from salt air, and transported it by barge to the port of Hamburg. The hollow bronze weighs six tons. On the 14th of July it left Germany on the Finnclipper of the Finnlines, and it arrived at Twenty-first Street in Brooklyn on July 30. Trucks deposited it at the uncompleted North Plaza of Lincoln Center on August 3, where it awaited Moore's arrival. It had previous survived an attack by Newbold Morris, Parks Commissioner for the city, who tried to prevent its installation, together with the installation of an Alexander Calder two hundred feet away. (A Lippold looks out from Philharmonic Hall at Moore's Reclining Figure; elsewhere are sculptures by Lipchitz, Bourdelle and Rodin.) The city's Arts Commission approved the sculptures by a five-to-four vote.

Moore flew from Rome to New York on Monday, August 23, and found the pool unprepared. Black tile was to cover the lead bottom of the pool—the color makes the water look deeper—but it had twice been laid and twice removed. Water had leaked through tiles and lead

Moore carving on vacation in Italy

into the offices underneath. Since the bottom of the pool was now merely lead, which is soft and easy to puncture, the sculpture and the superstructure for lifting the sculpture had to be placed on broad slats of wood at all times. Tuesday and Wednesday Moore (and Noack, who had flown over from Berlin) had virtually nothing to do. Interviewers and photographers and official people buzzed around him; at a camera session Thursday afternoon—the torso still in its crate—the clicking of shutters sounded like crickets in a hayfield. The workmen seemed more interested in the cameramen than in working, and frequently obscured sections of the foot part, which had progressed to the pool, with an advertisement for their company.

Moore went to dinner Thursday with officials and the donors, Mr. and Mrs. Albert A. List. When he returned to the North Plaza at ten o'clock, the sculpture was standing reasonably in place, lights playing on it from buildings on each side. He was overjoyed, and walked around and around the sculpture smiling happily. "Yes, I think that will *do*." Earlier in the day he had been worrying that it wasn't going to be big enough, and had arranged with Gordon Bunshaft (who designed the theater next to the pool) to raise the sculpture a little higher in the water. (The bronze goes only four inches below the surface; concrete supports, tiled black, take it down eight inches to the bottom.) Now it looked right to him; it will be a piece of landscape, he said, in the middle of New York. He climbed a staircase to see how it looked from there. "Yes, it *does* look like a rock!"

He spent the weekend with Bunshaft, looked at the Reclining Figure again on Monday, and flew back to Italy. On September 21, only a few days after his return to Much Hadham, he was in New York again for the dedication.

The city was in the middle of an unprecedented drought, but water was necessary to the sculpture as Moore had conceived it. For $800 the Lincoln Center bought enough water to provide the Reclining Figure with a reflection. Moore arrived early at the plaza, and was pleased again to see the culmination of the work that had begun nearly four years earlier, when he had looked at the architect's plans in Much Hadham. The water was a touch stagnant, but it gave the sculpture back to itself, and doubled the semicircular space at the bottom of the torso, turning it into a circle. Musicians gathered at one corner of the plaza and played while the five hundred invited guests assembled. Cameras clicked around Moore, and interviewers held microphones to him. Old friends were in attendance too—Sir Kenneth Clark and Harry Fischer—and Joseph Hirshhorn kissed him on both cheeks.

A few minutes after four, Moore, the donors and other dignitaries filed onto a platform at one end of the pool. Other guests sat on folding chairs at the sides of the pool. William Schuman, President of Lincoln Center, started the program, which he called a launching rather than an unveiling. Platform-sitters who were not speaking—including John D. Rockefeller III and Newbold Morris himself—were introduced and stood up. Then Frank Stanton spoke briefly and elegantly, and Mayor Wagner (accepting the gift of the sculpture on behalf of the city, which owns the plaza) presented Moore with a "medallion for distinguished cultural achievement." In acceptance Moore made the briefest speech of all; it lasted twenty-five seconds. Then everyone retired to the air-conditioned Philharmonic Hall to drink champagne under the golden spars of Lippold's Orpheus and Apollo. By this time Newbold Morris, who had a good view of the Reclining Figure from the platform, confessed himself converted to it.

As the sculpture swoops out of the pool in the North Plaza, it is a composite of Moore's recent formal discoveries. The looming, strong torso began with the looming leg of the Reclining Figure of 1929, and the metaphor of woman as landscape is at least as old as 1935, but the Lincoln Center Reclining Figure is not merely a composite Henry Moore: it is the logical development, and the culmination, of the ideas of the years just preceding it. In the sharpness of the bent, rising torso it is like the Bone Figure of 1961. The two parts are in a mother and child relationship, the torso protecting the legs, but they are also, more dramatically than any other Moore sculpture, an image of huge distant landscape—the torso coming out of the water like a cliff, the legs rising like a stone island. The two pieces allow him, as he said of the immediate ancestors of 1959, "to relate the sculpture not more obviously, but more *naturally* to natural forms . . . it separates itself more easily, say, from being only a reclining figure. . . ." Yet it is clearly female as well. The hip bones and pelvis of the torso are crags and hollow caves, but they retain their sexual identity. If one looks for formal sources one can discern the landscapes of Monet, an ancient

171

Another view of the Lincoln Center Reclining Figure

Mayan sculpture, the waves of the sea, the rocky shore of Kent, a piece of bone and Adel Crag. What happened in the mind, over sixty years of form experience, rises from the shallow pool.

It is not only experience of forms, but of mothers and of all women, of sheltering and suffering, of the creation of life from the womb, and of the decay of the body in death. The sculpture *includes,* and changes as the light changes. By night, lighted from the new Metropolitan Opera building, it is another sculpture, or another series of sculptures. In any light, there are the abundance of forms revealed as the observer walks around it, the Protean nature of shapes; here a thigh, there a horizon. The eye flows from association to association, from a claw to a root to a face. Strange disparities grow from these associations: She is a whole body in the grave; her torso is the single bone of a huge body. She is an immovable cliff; she is a running figure. She is a piece of nature, as inclusive as nature. Like the greatest artists, Moore has the ability to reach in himself something like the mind of the baby for whom all things are one thing, and for whom miraculous transformations constantly occur: A breast turns into a yellow cat turns into a pillow turns into a sister turns into a tree. The psychically primitive has its parallels in the historically primitive; both include the conflicting extremes of love and death. This inclusiveness is the nature of Henry Moore's genius.

Index

INDEX

PICTURE CREDITS